Be on Your Way

SUSAN R. SCOTT

Copyright © 2020 Susan R. Scott

All rights reserved.

ISBN: 979-8-6384-7525-3

Unless otherwise indicated, all Scripture taken from the
HOLY BIBLE, NEW INTERNATIONAL VERSION ®.
Copyright © 1973, 1978, 1984 by International Bible Society.
Used by permission of Zondervan Publishing House.
All rights reserved.

To my lifelong traveling companion, my husband, Steve ~

I'm so grateful God chose YOU to be on this journey with me. Not only have you made this trip doable, you have made it

… the adventure of a lifetime!

CONTENTS

Dedication iii
Acknowledgements vii
INTRODUCTION: Where To? 1
CHAPTER 1: Is it Too Soon to Pack? 7
CHAPTER 2: What's Gray and has a Trunk? 19
CHAPTER 3: Why Do We Do This Again? 27
CHAPTER 4: Are We There Yet? 37
CHAPTER 5: How About We Sing a Song? 47
CHAPTER 6: Which Way is Up? 57
CHAPTER 7: How Far Can We Get on Fumes? 69
CHAPTER 8: Is There Any Other Way? 79
CHAPTER 9: Do You Have a Reservation? 89
CHAPTER 10: Are You Hungry Yet? 99
CHAPTER 11: Is it Time to Stretch? 111
CHAPTER 12: Wait, What Did That Say? 121
CONCLUSION: Is This It? 133
About the Author 141

Acknowledgements

I would like to acknowledge and thank my 12-year-old grandson, **Elijah**, for making my vision come to life by skillfully creating with connecting blocks the church-on-wagon-wheels pictured on the cover. Great job, Eli! Thanks for your willingness to help, for being so patient with me, and for making it so fun.

Kimberlyn Evers, your feedback, honest opinions, and technical help are invaluable to me. Thank you for faithfully coming to my rescue time and again. I love and appreciate you, and not just because you're my daughter.

Shawn Downes, you are so good at what you do. Thank you for all your editing suggestions and notes. I take full responsibility for any of the correkshuns you marked that I might have mist. [I guess I should have you edit the acknowledgement page next time, huh?]

My sincerest thanks and love to **my prayer-warrior friends**, *who were on call and willing to pray whenever my ears-to-hear got blocked. You made completing this book possible!*

INTRODUCTION: Where To?

How many times have we wished for a book or a download, a method of other people's success stories — something to grab onto as we float aimlessly like a dandelion seed desperately looking for fertile soil — hoping for a shift in wind direction, something to direct us so we can finally find our destined place to put down roots? This is not that book. In fact, I'm writing this from midair for anyone else not sure of where the "wind of change" is blowing them, to let you know there are many of us not sure where God is headed. But we know He's on the move. And as He passes us, we will swirl in behind Him to follow His lead. Unlike moves of God in the past which affected pockets of believers, I believe this move of God is mobilizing His entire worldwide congregation.

Picture His Church like a field of dandelions, with deep roots, being swayed by the wind. There are some of us who have already gone to seed, detached from our roots and feeling quite exposed and

INTRODUCTION: Where To?

vulnerable, just waiting and hoping for the others to go to seed as well so we won't feel so awkward. Meanwhile, here we float, desperately watching for God to give us some direction or at least some affirmation.

I woke up one morning (well halfway awake anyhow) with my eyes still closed but aware of being conscious, and I had a clear dream-like vision of a little white church-building (steeple and all) set on four wagon wheels. As it rolled past me left to right, I heard a voice inside me say, "Be on your way."

I asked, "Be on my way where?"

"That's the title of your next book, *Be on Your Way*."

"But my first book isn't published yet."

Then I heard God tell me it was mine to write and He'd give me what I needed. He spoke it to me in poetry form and I knew I couldn't come up with a rhyme that quickly, especially half asleep. He let me know it wasn't just my imagination.

> *Be on your way into the night. Don't fear the dark.*
> *I'll be your Light. Just close your eyes, I'll give you sight.*
> *Open your heart. Begin to write.*

Then I woke up and found a pen and scribbled it down. When I was done, the next part flowed onto the paper. Please bear in mind I hadn't had my first cup of tea yet:

Be on Your Way

It's you I've called to do this thing for Me.
You're just the one to bring the word that's waiting
in the wing. Now take the mic and start to sing.

"I despise singing into microphones, but I'll do it if I have to."

"No, Honey, it's a metaphor."

"Oh." Then I heard,

Be on your way, leave all behind.
Take only with you heart and mind.

"Okay, I get it. Don't look back. But, God, I have nothing to say. I have no idea where You're even taking us. How can I write about how to get there?"

No need to plan or orchestrate. Come to the stove with empty plate.
I'll fill it up. Be still and wait. Savor it. Then go create. Polished like an
arrow in the shadow of My hand; Made to claim my Kingdom back.
It's time for you to stand ... and be on your way.

"I don't know, God, I don't think this introduction will capture anyone's attention. Don't I need a little more to kick start this thing?"

Don't worry. The people this is meant for will keep reading anyhow.

"But some profound thoughts or a few inspired gems to set this apart from just pages of an old journal wouldn't hurt, don't You think? Hey, like maybe You could make *Be on Your Way* an invaluable stepping stone for those of us stuck in a holding pattern? Maybe You could

INTRODUCTION: Where To?

reveal to us what our next assignments will be and how to get there? I have no idea where this is going, but alright, I'll start writing just because You said to."

This book is me surrendering to God's best intentions for me, rhyming confirmations and all. I've learned He never tells me to do anything that isn't beneficial or somehow rewarding (maybe embarrassing, but beneficial nonetheless). And if I want to see world change, I have to let Him change me and how I see the world first.

At this moment I have no clue where we're headed, but you're welcome to come along if you like a mystery. You may have picked up this book simply because of the title. You've been sensing those words too, and something inside is talking back, "On my way to where?" I think the "where" may be our destiny. Not just our individual destinies, but more so our divine destiny as a family of humanity in unison, in step with our Creator. It's time to do what we were created for, what God has prepared us for in this past crazy-hard season (for some, a lifelong season). It's time to go for it, and go for it with our whole heart, no holding back.

But go for what? It would be helpful to at least find out what "it" is, don't you think? And what in the world does a picture of a church on wheels have to do with anything (other than making for an interesting minimalistic book cover)? Could it be that we're all in this together? We are all designed and gifted to be part of "being Jesus" to the people who don't know Him yet, and to those who do. We are called His Body, His Bride: The Church. But it's going to take *all* of us going in the same direction to affectively impact the insanity of darkness surrounding us right now. Those of us waiting for the others to catch on have been given a head start — God knows why. We could be the leaders, or maybe we're just slower and we needed a head start — extra time to change our thinking.

I think I'm writing this to you. If you're breathing right now, you are part of God's plan to save humanity and see God's Kingdom come and His will to be done on Earth as it is in Heaven. Even if we find ourselves floating, God assures us that we were born on purpose to complete our unique assignments. But all our assignments are supernaturally intertwined; we can't afford to try to do this by ourselves, as segmented denominations, or subdivisions of our denominations. God has something totally different in mind and He's about to download His strategy, not just to me, but to you too, and everyone else with ears to hear. We are very much in this together.

Far from being about all the "wrongness" of past church experiences and the new and improved "rightness" of a cleverly designed method of "being the church," I think God might be leading me to write this book to try to teach us how to unite and find commonality, a bond to strengthen us during this transition into unknown territory. Like pioneers trusting in wagon wheels to move us onward, ours is the story of stepping out, moving on, going someplace else, but like Abraham, having no idea where that someplace actually is. We have heard God's invitation to share in the adventure. With it comes the challenge of waiting, watching, not

INTRODUCTION: Where To?

looking back, and then letting go and jumping in when it's time. He'll tell us when.

If you're like me, you know how tempting it is to look backwards and recall all your mistakes and failures (sometimes in hopes of finding an excuse not to move forward). You wouldn't want to endure the embarrassment, awkwardness, and consequences of making the same mistakes again. But by dwelling on the past, we are reliving those difficult feelings anyhow and, in the process, we are blocking the new blessings of what God has in store for us. Everything that has happened thus far has brought us to this threshold, this launching pad. Good, bad, or ugly, without the past mistakes we would not have been made ready for this moment — this, God's finest moment for us. So, don't get tangled in the caution tape.

Look, we're still here. Even after everything we've been through, we're still here — near to the Father's heart. Having tested and tasted, stumbled and fumbled through, we have decided our Father's heart beats stronger than anything in our past, and stronger than all our differences.

He is moving so quickly; we may have to run to catch up with this movement of His. He is supernaturally readying Jesus' Bride (that's us) for the return of her King! My hope is by the end of this book you and I will be encouraged and have some personal strategy or revelation to inspire us forward, united together —

no matter what "be on your way" may mean.

CHAPTER 1: Is it Too Soon to Pack?

Maybe it's a good idea to unpack from the last trip first. I think that's what this interim of us floating around has been for. We're seeing things from a different perspective. We are feeling the difference between stability and mobility, and we're discovering that being mobile isn't necessarily an unstable way to live.

A lot of my stability came from being part of an established church community throughout my life. My faith was formed and sustained in a conservative, consistent, weekly gathering. Not committing to one local church body or not pouring heart and soul into the ministry there, was frowned upon, even scolded, in my neck of the woods. But somehow here we are: loving and serving God and not committed to any one particular congregation — opposite of everything we had been promoting by example for all these years. Taking away any life pattern

CHAPTER 1: Is it Too Soon to Pack?

can cause a sense of imbalance. To find ourselves in this very "opposite" and uncomfortable place with others dizzily floating beside us, leads me to believe that there is a move of God happening that's bigger than all of us combined. Or could it be that's exactly what He's trying to do — combine us all?

For decades God has been stirring the nest. When it's time for her eaglets to fly, a mother eagle actually rearranges the twigs of a nest to point inward so the eaglets get so uncomfortable they are forced to spread their wings and jump. God is helping us snuggly-safe congregants find that the option to stay as is or move on, isn't quite so optional. He is purposely kicking us into our fly-or-be-stuck-by-pointy-sticks phase. Sticks that imply "be on your way." It's time to pry your tightened little bird-feet off everything you've known so far (or think you've known), leaving your wings open to new possibilities. It's time to start flapping.

There was nothing wrong with that old thinking; it was everything you needed for the last trip. Things left in the suitcase from a weekend excursion and mistakenly put away in the back of the closet for months don't cause any real harm. The suitcase may get dust-covered, the clothes wrinkly and a bit musty, but it's nothing laundering can't fix (unless we're talking about a damp towel that got left unpacked, in which case you may have to throw out the whole suitcase). Still, everything you brought, including the stinky towel, served its purpose at the time and was needed for that particular trip.

Be on Your Way

If God is really re-forming His Bride, is there anything about the way we have "done church" He can recycle? Is there anything about my life-long church experience I would want to take with me as I pack my bags and be on my way? God is going to have to reveal this one to me. It's all just too dust-covered. I may have even left a damp towel in there somewhere.

I know that we learn from mistakes and we try not to repeat them, but I don't want to be critical of traditions and missions that have been precious and dear to me in the past (and still are very important to many people who have good hearts and pure motives). Falling into old patterns because they come easily and feel familiar can really squash a new design and fresh start, so it's important to recognize past patterns that may not be helpful to new revelations. Jesus talked about not pouring new wine into old wineskins. As the wine ages it stretches the wineskin to its maximum capacity. The wineskin has successfully served its purpose, but cannot be used again for new wine because it has no more "give" left in it. It would simply burst.

Floating out here has given us a chance to observe a few things about our own thinking and methods as well as what we see happening in churches of well-meaning believers. Not wanting to replicate what felt like shortcomings or mistakes in our past ministry paradigms can leave a room full of Church re-forming novices voicing critical opinions, pointing to all the stretch marks of our past birthing experiences. And really, it is not very helpful.

CHAPTER 1: Is it Too Soon to Pack?

Instead, I believe there's great value and importance in remembering God's faithfulness in our past wilderness experiences. It's recounting His deeds of old, His gracious and miraculous provision, guidance, and protection that get us ready, that open us up to new wine, new ideas and techniques. Or maybe, just possibly, remembering them will make us ready to embrace some very, very old methods — ancient ways tried and true, God's original design, rebirthed and updated for a time such as this.

Transition is the most intense part of labor. Everything leading up to it is just a walk in the park compared to it, or so I've been told. I was an epidural, stop-the-madness kind of woman. Keeping ourselves free from pain is a natural instinct. But sometimes fear of pain can control us. Only when we want an outcome more than we want to be pain-free do we take the plunge. We throw off the comfy towel of safety and cannonball into the deep end (I shuttered just typing it). You see, I don't plunge; I dangle. Sometimes, I may dare to splash my arms in the frigid, icy, June water if it's a hot enough day. But it has to be a treacherously hot, muggy, hard-to-breathe August before I'm desperate enough to wade incrementally into the shallow end. Then after adjusting, I plunge my head under just long enough to get my hair damp. And I call it "courageous." All that to help you understand that this time of uncertainty, this floating without direction, makes me feel both uncomfortable and wrapped in a towel of safety at the same time.

I want what I do and say to make a splash, to have meaning and purpose. That can only happen if I'm fully relying on God. When something becomes too familiar and easy, there's not a lot of "trusting God" to make it happen. It's hard to obey Proverbs 3:6 and "lean *not* on your own understanding" when you know just how to do something with no real effort needed.

God knows I feel more comfortable when I have a predictable, scheduled consistency to my spiritual-community gatherings (church). Waiting for the unpredictable, not knowing when or where God will say, "Okay now! Dive in!" makes me ask, "Was my old familiar way of doing church really so bad? It seems to be working for everybody else."

There was nothing wrong with my old thinking when it was new. It served a purpose. It was part of the building blocks that got me here. I'm not about to knock down *your* tower. I'm just saying that for me, building-blocks-lover that I am, seeing how high a tower I can construct before I run out of blocks is really fun. But just as fun for me is taking a picture of my tower swaying in the breeze first, and then strategically pulling out one of the pivotal blocks near the bottom and watching all the wooden blocks come crashing down, loudly clanking together like a victory cry! If it happens prematurely or accidentally while building, it's frustrating and feels like I've failed somehow. But when it's on my terms, in my timing, by my choice, it proves very satisfying indeed.

You have to deconstruct before you can reconstruct. Only this time, maybe by adding new blocks and a slightly sturdier design, you can build higher than ever. Using all the old blocks as the foundation

CHAPTER 1: Is it Too Soon to Pack?

is what makes a new, higher tower possible. There's nothing wrong with them; it's just time to take it to the next level by adding new blocks. But I guess this is where my building blocks metaphor gets a bit unsteady.

Now for anyone who has been (or currently is) involved in a "seeker-sensitive" church service, what I'm about to write is in no way meant to insult or criticize. In fact, I was deeply involved in the creative process of producing and executing a seeker-sensitive service every Sunday for 15 years. I know our heart and mission was to present the gospel message weekly, especially to friends and visitors who didn't like going to "normal church," or who had been hurt by "bad" church experiences. We would deliver a timeless message to a broken people in a contemporary, calm, relaxed, and entertaining way. We gave them a taste of how fun church could be. We didn't want people to sing anything they didn't mean, so the choruses would be light and generic, but would somehow fit with the theme for that day. Then there would be special music performed for them by gifted musicians, and a dramatic or comedic sketch that presented the message further. I was responsible for writing or finding the sketch that was performed every week to set up the sermon (like a sermon illustration, but live).

Back in the early 1990s this was cutting edge. We prayed a lot before introducing the concept to a very traditional congregation. Together, we withstood the kick-back of the "boo-birds" (those not in favor of such a radical mission), and felt all that much more determined to go against the grain of rituals and traditions. The lessons and transformations were astounding, and we knew it wasn't our doing. It was totally God! I know our motivation was to resuscitate people who had been beaten down by a religious spirit, and the immediate results we saw encouraged us. Using our creative talents to offer a seeker-service had breathed new life into our own lives as well. But I also witnessed 20 years later the long-term results — they were not as glorious. Our good intentions had fed into the already culturally-present consumer mentality. We had bypassed the holiness and reverence, and catered to the friendly and non-threatening, easy as 1,2,3, repeat after me.

It was a pendulum swing for sure. And I now see it was one that had to happen to ready us for where God is about to take His Church next. But like a parent who was abused in childhood trying to overcompensate as they raise their own children — indulging, hovering, and overparenting — we created a generation of uncommitted, church-of-convenience goers. We unwittingly taught them, "Church is all about *you!*" We even gave them a 7-point checklist for church-shopping:

1. Does it meet all my needs (support groups, programs, potlucks, etc.)?
2. Is there easy, convenient parking?
3. Are people friendly and welcoming?
4. How is the music? Too loud? Too slow?
5. Is the preacher engaging, relevant, and funny?

CHAPTER 1: Is it Too Soon to Pack?

    6. Do they get me out on time?

And the one that really adds a sense of spirituality to the list:

    7. Does God show up? [translation: Do I feel warm and fuzzy?]

We've also made sure that people know they don't need to stick around if they're offended in any way, especially by being scolded (held accountable). They can just give leadership a "Hmph! Well I never!" grab their checklist, and stomp their way off to a more suitable, less demanding church.

I can remember looking at the coffee-cup-holding worshipers, bopping to the catchy tunes as they talked over the music to their friends a couple rows ahead about where they were going for lunch, and thinking to myself, "What have we done? We've created a church-consuming monster!"

If you attract people with quality entertainment and comfortable surroundings, you have to keep it up to keep them coming back. Every Easter and Christmas when the special effects and dramatic presentations were especially impactful, I can remember thinking, "How are we going to top this next year?" Planning a Sunday morning worship service had become all about serving the people — loving and teaching them in a way that would keep them coming back. At the time it felt right, but my job became keeping them in the Kingdom by keeping them comfortable and happy. If we gave them a performance to which they were proud to bring their friends, that was practically like teaching them how to evangelize.

Be on Your Way

God has had to pry my little bird feet off of something I knew how to create and do in my sleep and reveal to me HIS original strategy to demonstrate His love to His wandering children. The importance and real impact made by God's powerful signs, wonders, and miracles, convince and invite people not necessarily into a church gathering, but into their loving Father's Kingdom. I had lived and breathed with the mistaken idea that my church *was* the Kingdom of God. By bringing people into our church I felt I was giving them the best chance to pray a prayer of salvation and become part of God's Kingdom. And as the numbers attending grew, I mistakenly calculated that as Kingdom growth.

As God's Holy Spirit began to show us, and teach us, about the authority we have (over the darkness), and the power that the Name of Jesus carries, we realized that God's supernatural gifts of prophecy, words of knowledge, and the healing gifts, worked better for us than any apologetics' method when it came to proving God's love. Don't get me wrong: knowing the truth of God's Word and having an answer for the hope that is within us is just as important. It's just that our eyes were opened wider to the long-term effects of ministry as we knew it, and it sent us on our way to search and find what God wanted us to discover next.

See, we've been here before. Not knowing exactly where we're headed, feeling like a person without a country, is nothing new. I'm sure you have been there before too. It's moments like these that test and strengthen our faith.

CHAPTER 1: Is it Too Soon to Pack?

I know there will come a day when our faith will become sight, and all our senses will be supernaturally increased. Then, everything we think we now know will be up for re-thinking all over again. Because faith pleases God, I believe that when that day comes there will still be room for even more faith to grow. Faith simply means we believe in God's Character more than in our senses (even heavenly, supernatural senses). Believing Him is trusting Him, and trusting Him is an act of love.

Even though hearing "be on your way" can feel like an unwelcome change, faith hears it beckoning a new beginning and a new way. Yes, change can be scary, but it invites new ideas and new stories to be part of our telling. History may repeat itself, but when the players are new, the outcome of the game is being influenced differently, so even winning (or losing) can be at a whole new level.

The calendar is based on cycles and changing positions of heavenly bodies, and we have absolutely no say about it. But things in the spiritual heavenlies *can* be influenced by our faith-filled prayers and declarations. That realm has shifted and the spiritual gravitational pull is what has caused many of us to sense the imminent change at hand. It's bigger than our resistance to it.

Time to take a deep breath and look over the edge. Let brave hearts play with the impossibilities that only God can (and will) make possible. That shimmer of hope sparkling in front of you is not a mirage. Dare to entertain its beauty and celebrate the nearness of the next venture. Let time fly out the window. Rest in eternity and its limitlessness. Don't think you're setting yourself up for disappointment or failure. You're simply opening your arms up to amazing blessings and something much bigger on a whole new level.

Maybe the new blocks we need to use are much older than we think. Maybe we need to think archeologically. Could it be that ancient blocks, truly foundational but sadly forgotten and buried, are actually the ones we need to unearth and add on to form the next level? Maybe we should ditch the suitcase and pull down the old antique trunk from the attic. Moving forward sometimes means first stepping back to gain the necessary momentum needed to take that leap. Step back and recount God's deeds of old: His faithfulness and miraculous provision, His guidance and protection. Focus on all of that to ready yourself and open yourself to the new wine. There's so much to discover. And there's lots and lots of new mistakes to make, new lessons to learn, and chances to fail and see God's grace pick us back up again. It's all okay. Our past has equipped us like hockey goalies. We may still feel the impact of the puck, but it won't leave a mark this time.

Remember God's past faithfulness and bring it with you to this moment. Let it help you focus on what's right in front of you. Living in the moment is different than living *for* the moment. It is not about living without thinking consequentially. It's more about thinking of eternal consequences beyond just the fleeting ones.

CHAPTER 1: Is it Too Soon to Pack?

There is definitely purpose in the waiting. It feels to me like it's positioning us to soon toss the towels, link arms, and together courageously run to the edge:

One, two, three ... Cannonball!

CHAPTER 2: What's Gray and has a Trunk?

I know "a mouse going on vacation" is an old joke (so old I couldn't exactly remember the punch line) but it still made me smile when my husband gave me the answer. Obviously, I'm not an elephant because as we all know, "elephants never forget."

There are only two other elephant adages I can remember: "There's an elephant in the room that no one wants to talk about," and the one referring to the parable of the blind men trying to describe to each other an elephant in front of them but experiencing just the one part of the elephant that they can feel — trunk, ear, leg, side, tail, tusk. Clearly without being able to see the whole elephant, they each have completely different viewpoints. This ancient parable has taken on many different endings — some violent, some cooperative and

CHAPTER 2: What's Gray and has a Trunk?

harmonious. I like harmony, where each person listens to the other, putting their descriptive experiences together to form the big picture.

I remember learning from my high school art teacher how to enlarge a photo or drawing by hand simply by breaking it into a grid of squares and then looking at one small square at a time and then recreating each square onto a bigger square one by one. You could assign a whole class the project, each person drawing only one of the squares. And then, like a mosaic, you'd put the squares together to create a really cool blown-up version of the original.

God wants us to work together on His HUGE project of captivating nations with the Love of Father God. He has given us our assignments, our small squares of influence, and the inspired stories and instructions in the Bible as a blueprint to follow. But we only need to focus on and expand our small part. He's asking us to trust His exquisite timing, vision, and purpose. Even if your little square seems insignificant to you, He is waiting patiently for you to complete it. Because without it, His perfectly detailed vision can't be realized.

Sometimes we can feel like everybody else has a big important assignment, and what we do couldn't possibly be as vital. After all, look at all the "big names" having such a giant impact. Surely their squares are all that really count. My drawing might as well be done on the inside of a cave wall somewhere. I'm the only one who's going to see it anyway.

Be on Your Way

There was a battle to be fought before the Israelites claimed the land promised to them by God. They had to put into practice what they had learned for 40 years of their lives living independently of their former Egyptian masters, but living completely dependent on God. Their parents had felt insignificant, and forgetting God, they believed that the giants (literal giants) standing in their way were too big for them. Only Joshua and Caleb, who believed God was bigger and would give them victory, were allowed to enter the promised land ... but 40 years later. It took 40 years going around the same mountain for the doubters to die off. It was finally time for all the "little people" to unite, tribe by tribe, under the leadership and faith of those two men. Trusting God, they fought for what was promised to them, despite how impossible it looked.

About 360 years later, David (before becoming king) found himself hiding in a cave with 400 outcasts of society as their present king, Saul, was trying out of jealousy to hunt David down to kill him. But that sense of belonging and being valued under the leadership of an anointed soon-to-be king did something in those men that made them warriors who were prepared, not scared. They became, and were known as David's "mighty men of valor."

I've heard many prophetic voices declaring lately that leaders and "mighty people of valor" are about to step out of the shadowy caves of preparation into the spotlight of recognition — like a secret weapon designed, prepared, and tested, concealed in a backroom, but now ready to be released. Are you one of those leaders? One of those

CHAPTER 2: What's Gray and has a Trunk?

seemingly insignificant squares? Am I? Have you been in a cave-like place, a wilderness of your own, where you're waiting on God for everything? He's invested in you, trained you, and made you feel like you belong and that you matter. But you don't know quite what to do with yourself now. You're waiting for instructions of what the rest of your square is supposed to look like and how it fits in.

When enlarging a picture by hand, an important part of the process is having a number on the back of each assigned square to be able to easily reassemble the picture when ready. God has designed us each to receive and give, compliment and connect. Our Heavenly Father, our Creator, is the One who put the numbers on the back of our squares. He also numbered the very hairs on our heads, and named each star in the sky as He placed them in their perfect order. He really knows what He's doing! But if your number is higher or lower than someone else's, you can't interpret that your square is any more or any less important. And don't be so concerned with what everybody else is drawing. If you're trying to copy them, your square is not going to fit into God's design very well. So stop comparing; this is not a competition. It's a cooperative effort and it takes every one, every square — even yours. Without *your* square the mosaic cannot be completed.

When it's time to reassemble us, and we're squirming and resisting where God wants us to go because we obviously aren't wholeheartedly trusting Him, He may have to put us to the side for a bit (like a time-out) until we're ready to let Him place us where He knows we fit best. It feels like my husband and I, even though we thought we were listening, have been set aside for the moment. It's hard to believe that this was part of God's plan, with all the pain of leaving the familiar behind and the scary prospect of having to get comfortable again in new surroundings. But from over here on the sidelines, we are being given a new perspective — a different side of the elephant to feel.

The frustration of observing "church consumerism" from the inside out has been eating at us for a while now. God has set us out here to grow our limbs back (like gingerbread cookies that got dunked too many times trying to be Jesus's hands and feet). By graciously placing us where we are for now, God is giving us a chance to look from the outside in, and not just outside a church building to observe "here's the church, here's the steeple, open the doors and see all the people." He's also taken us outside of ourselves so we can look within our own hearts and minds at our weaknesses, tendencies, and motives.

We heard a teaching on spiritual gifts that helped us embrace this awkward time-out. We've known right along that we both have been given a heart to shepherd people. We found out that what we thought was one of our weaknesses is actually a common challenge of that gift. What we learned was that because a shepherd's heart is all about caring for, feeding, loving, and unfortunately, pleasing people, shepherds can be easily manipulated by critical bleating and complaining. They are tender toward peoples' needs and brokenness, and can become weary chasing after all the wanderers, catering to some pretty unrealistic

CHAPTER 2: What's Gray and has a Trunk?

demands. That's why we're weary. It is not a job for just one or two people.

Too many "incognito pastors" sit quietly in a congregation not understanding that their calling is shepherding too, even though they have no degree or title, and they don't "run the church." Nor does their call and gifting include preaching or administration. But because of our church-corporation paradigm, these gifted-by-God shepherds aren't recognized because they don't meet CEO standards. Meanwhile, the pastor in the pulpit may not have shepherding skills at all. He or she may strictly be a teacher, or evangelist, or prophet, maybe even an apostle, with leadership skills, who is so focused on preparing for Sunday (the one time a week they get to use their true gift and communicate their heart to the whole flock) that wandering or missing sheep are not being chased after.

And within that said flock, there are teachers, apostles, and prophets who are hearing revelation straight from Heaven and are being forced to sit quietly in their seats and nod politely at someone's diligently crafted 40-minute dissertation, because after all, that's what the pastor is being paid to do. Even though these gifted children of God are being nudged to add to the speech, or maybe even correct something they hear, that's the pastor up there, for crying out loud. This is neither the time nor the place. Or is it?

Isn't that what God intended for us to do by creating us to thrive in community? He's given us each other to run things by, correct, encourage, and complete. We live life together, mature ones imparting what they've learned to young ones, everyone helping each other through challenges, celebrating each other's blessings and triumphs, and experiencing others' joys and sorrows as if they were our own.

Please hear my heart: this is not about rebelling against authority. The Bible teaches us to respect church leaders, teachers, overseers, deacons, and apostles. God tells us to submit to one another and to financially bless those who minister to us. We are to respect wise counsel and be accountable while holding others accountable with great patience and humility.[1] I'm simply suggesting that overseeing a homestead of gifted believers who are living life to bring God's Kingdom to earth is a whole lot more than just a one-shepherd job. Wouldn't it make sense to spread out that kind of responsibility to a team of apostles, prophets, evangelists, teachers, pastors, healers and miracle workers? God seems to think so, too:

> And God has placed in the church first of all apostles, second prophets, third teachers, then miracles, then gifts of healing, of helping, of guidance and of different kinds of tongues (1 Corinthians 12:28).

> So Christ Himself gave the apostles, the prophets, the evangelists, the pastors and teachers, to equip His people for works of service, so that the body of Christ may be built up until we all reach *unity* in the faith and in the knowledge of the Son of God and become

---

[1] 1 Thessalonians 5:12-13, Hebrews 13:17, 1 Peter 5:5, 1 Timothy 5:17-18, and 2 Timothy 4:2

CHAPTER 2: What's Gray and has a Trunk?

mature, attaining to the whole measure of the fullness of Christ… From Him the whole body, joined and held together by every supporting ligament, grows and builds itself up in love, *as each part does its work* (Ephesians 4:11-13&16, *emphasis mine*).

What then shall we say, brothers and sisters? When you come together, *each of you* has a hymn, a word of instruction, revelation, a tongue or an interpretation. Everything must be done so that the church may be built up (1 Corinthians 14:26, *emphasis mine*).

So here I sit, scribbling down words that I hope will help pick up all the spilled popcorn and somehow scrape off the stepped-on, sticky candy that feels permanently stuck to the sanctuary floor. The confetti cannons were impressive and created a moment, but now I can't find the push broom. I helped create the mess. I can't expect someone else to clean it up, nor can I do it alone.

Maybe that's what God is giving me to write down — a cry for help, a call to arms, or maybe just a book of key questions that might help open the door to the broom closet —

or maybe even unlock the ancient ways
stored in the attic trunk.

CHAPTER 3: Why Do We Do This Again?

It seems like every time I go away to get a change of scene, even for a few days, I end up asking that same question: Why? Because after the hours of angst over what to bring and what not to bring and trying to fit half the house into the car, riding uncomfortably in a car full of half the house for however long, having to first hunt for and then use less-than-sanitary facilities, finding the least disgusting restaurants off the nearest exits, eating every meal of who-knows-what prepared (who knows how?) by who-knows-who, sleeping (mostly not sleeping) on a torturous mattress, and paying out more than a mortgage payment to stay in a room with such thin walls I get to know my vacation neighbors much better than I'd ever like to — after all that, I come home to the mess and responsibilities I left behind trying to scramble out the door (hoping to beat the traffic on my way to a "glorious get-away") and I end up sitting amongst the piles of dirty vacation clothes,

CHAPTER 3: Why Do We Do This Again?

unwanted mail, and "urgent" messages, shaking my head, dazed and wondering who in the world invented vacation and what could they have possibly been thinking? How many times have you heard yourself say, "I need a vacation to recover from vacation"? The very thing that is supposed to refresh, renew, and inspire us onward, instead frustrates, depletes, and leaves us feeling cheated.

Somehow, as time passes, the vacation memories blur and morph in our heads and start looking more like one of the postcard pictures we saw in that exorbitantly-overpriced souvenir shop. And for some reason we start planning — and actually looking forward to — our next trip. There's just no explaining why we do some of the things we do.

Case in point: Back in ancient times (the 1960s when I was a kid), there was a fading, but persistent, tradition called the "Sunday Afternoon Drive." There was no particular destination, rhyme, or reason that I could see from a kid's-eye view anyhow. It was just what families did. You'd pile in the car, start it up, back out of the driveway, and go.

Sometimes we kids were bribed with the promise of ice cream or a stop at the giant slide in the park on the way home if we'd "just get in the car and be quiet for even a minute." It was a parental 2-for-1 bribe: 1. It got us in the car. And 2. "Stop fighting or I'll turn this car around" had a lot more clout if missing out on ice cream or the park slide was at stake.

Be on Your Way

Sometimes the ride felt so long that napping in the back seat was inevitable. The thought of seeing a horse or spotting an old stone wall to walk on might keep us alert for a bit, but the possibility that kept us the most awake was the rollercoaster road bumps (those places in the road where you speed up to go over the next rise in the road, then ease up on the gas pedal and lose your stomach as you sink back down over the other side). We loved those. So did my dad. My mom? Not so much.

Two other games that made the ride bearable were "Left, Right, Left" (just turning down which ever street was to the left, and then taking the next right, then the next left, etc.) and my favorite: "Wonder Where This Road Goes." My dad and I thought it was adventurous. My mom? Again, not so much. She got claustrophobic and really nervous when the houses and power lines disappeared (this was way before cell phones and navigator systems). My older sister just acted bored, but I think she may have been picking up on my mother's anxiety and only complaining "it was boring" so my dad would turn around. But somewhere in the Sunday Afternoon Adventurers' Handbook (at least my dad's copy) it stated that turning around is not an option. Onward and upward! Always forward! Never back up! Never surrender! (to the road, that is). I guess I just really trusted that my dad knew how to get us home. And I kind of liked not knowing where I was, with someone who (I at least thought) *did* know. It's exciting to explore new places with someone you trust.

CHAPTER 3: Why Do We Do This Again?

But the part when the way forward inevitably turned into a cow path was a good indication that the road was about to win this one. My dad had the uncanny knack of finding every dead-end street within driving distance that our town's Department of Public Works forgot to post. It became such a phenomenon that we had to start bribing my *mom* with ice cream to get her into the car. Turning around in the middle of nowhere with two children in the back seat, at the end of the dirt road with ditches and drop offs (again no cell phones and miles from help if we ever got stuck) turned my mother's anxiety into pure panic. "Paul Frederick, I will never get into this car with you again!" That is, until the next Sunday when it was time for the ritual drive, and the homemade ice cream was calling louder than the threatening dead-end ditch. Ah, yes ... the ancient days.

Now move ahead to the olden days (the early 1980's) when in our twenties we discovered (announcement trumpet please) Da-ta-ta-dah: Auto Clubs! They not only rescued you on the road if you broke down close enough to a pay phone, but they generously provided special turn-by-turn directions to your destination, with highlighted maps and highly-coveted discounted hotel coupons. My sister worked at one of those agencies, so when on a whim, my husband, sister, and I decided to play hooky one Friday to go on a road trip from Massachusetts to Pennsylvania and visit some friends, she put together one of those new-fangled "direction packages" for us. There was none of the "left, right, left" game or "wonder where this road goes," but there were a lot of ice cream stops. We were all going to a place we'd never been before. It was bold and spontaneous, and it was fun! We took off from a routine Friday, and just followed our heart ... and the fancy highlighted-maps.

Maybe this phase of life we're in, and hearing "be on your way," is stirring up these memories for me for obvious reasons. I'm hoping you've been able to sense where I'm going with this. Simply: There are times we don't understand the real purpose behind what we're doing or even why we keep doing something we don't really enjoy, over and over and over again. We end up doing something every Sunday, and making the best of it, but still not knowing why or how we got there.

Here we are piled in this car together, and we need each other's company to navigate our way through and have fun along the way. We don't know exactly where we are, but we trust our Dad to get us home. We understand that we can't play games this time. Hmm... the only thing we're missing is our "direction package." Oh! Wait a minute. What's this? It's the same blueprint we used (in Chapter 2) for drawing our squares! Well, what do you know?

The formation of the kind of community Jesus wants us to have can be observed most clearly in the early church documents and letters recorded in the blueprint of the Bible. It only makes sense that the very people who listened to Jesus, who knew Him in person or walked the earth when He was here as a Man, would have a fairly good idea of how God intends us to operate (and co-operate). Jesus trusted His followers who had studied and trained with Him for years to write down, or pass along by word of mouth, as many of His instructions

CHAPTER 3: Why Do We Do This Again?

and stories as they could remember. Each recalling what impressed them the most, they created a mosaic of Jesus' teachings and life — empowered and gifted by the Holy Spirit to communicate in supernatural ways, to speak and write exactly what God knew we would need to know then, as well as thousands of years later.

The blueprint we read about in the book of Acts isn't solely influenced and drawn by the culture of that day. It appears it was actually our Father's timeless design all along to have people gather like a family in intimate settings and share a meal, communion, songs, and stories. In even the first chapters of Scripture that capture the Creator's early interaction with His creation, we see God teaching us by walking and talking with us. As humanity grew, God assembled us into families and tribes, and instructed us through people who still walked with Him in awe. As mankind wandered away down the deadest of dead-end cow paths, our gracious Father lovingly set in place guideposts — feasts, festivals, customs, and rituals that pointed us and redirected us home. And then for thousands of years these customs sustained and encouraged God's people by pointing to their Deliverer (the Promised Messiah-King) through the rituals, gatherings, and mandated sacrifices. Animal sacrifices were a tangible act of repentance, like a visual aid to help us grasp the significance of what it takes to undo the damage done by our own prideful rebellion. Through God's kindness, He also required that the animals humanely sacrificed were deliciously prepared and then enjoyed together as a meal to be shared in God's Presence, like a family, reminding the worshipers of their Father's faithfulness, provision, and forgiveness.

He still points us back to the Old Covenant (Testament), to its prophetic words, its celebrations and promises, to help us understand the "why" of it all. The New Covenant God made with us (enacted by the Blood of Jesus on the Cross, and reenacted every time we take communion) confirms the validity of every prophetic word and commandment recorded in Scripture. Not only does Scripture accurately predict down to the minutest detail Jesus' first appearing, crucifixion and resurrection, but it also points us to His imminent return as the Jewish Messiah from the line of Judah, when He will rule and reign in this redeemed World, His Kingdom, forever from His throne in Jerusalem.

One might then ask: If we believe in and worship the Jewish Messiah, why aren't we all gathering in a synagogue to celebrate each Sabbath? Why don't we observe the feasts ordained by God that He said would be forever celebrated? Are any of our Sunday-morning/Saturday-evening traditions and rituals Scripturally based, or significant to *God*? Why do we do what we do again?

Just to be clear: Jesus is the unshakeable foundation and cornerstone of Christianity. Nothing can ever change that. But so much of what has been passed down to us are ages-worth of man-made traditions and superstitions. Not surprisingly, even some paganism can sneak its way into a belief system whose foundation of basic principles has been compromised. When and how was it compromised?

CHAPTER 3: Why Do We Do This Again?

The Jewish founders of Christianity already were part of a persecuted, over-ruled people. They were well accustomed to sticking together to survive and holding fast to their beliefs and traditions no matter what. Their Roman rulers were ruthless anti-Semites who tried to snuff them out. But the followers of Jesus were hated even more because even their fellow Jews thought they were blasphemers. And yet this relentless move of God to make disciples of all nations who would live in unity with Him, and harmony with each other, kept moving forward. Despite the giants that loomed before them, this Jewish remnant of courageous outcasts stood for the Truth ... and died for it as well.

Ephesians 2:14-16 tells us God's amazing plan:

For He Himself [Jesus] is our peace, who has made the two groups [Jew and Gentile] one and has destroyed the barrier, the dividing wall of hostility, by setting aside in His flesh the law with its commands and regulations. His purpose was to create in Himself one new humanity out of the two, thus making peace, and in one body to reconcile both of them to God through the cross, by which He put to death their hostility.

What in the world happened to *that* plan? The hostility between Jew and Gentile that had been buried by way of the Cross was unearthed by prejudice and greed, diminishing the richness of God's plan and postponing His purposes for the Church to become one new humanity, Jews and Gentiles united in Christ. It was the bigotry of a particular Roman ruler that compromised God's foundational plan for us by blinding many to the fact that the Romans were actually the agents who crucified Jesus, and then turned and blamed the Jews for making them do it (when in reality, *all* of humanity was responsible). It was the Roman emperor, Constantine the Great (ruling 306-337 AD), who legalized Christianity while decimating its Jewish roots.

Roman Catholicism was born at the expense of thousands of years of foundational history, teachings, and God-appointed feasts being dismissed. Constantine's zeal (fueled by his disdain for Judaism) to make Christianity the main religion of the Roman Empire may have gained Christians their freedom to worship above ground, but here's where the foundation was compromised: The significance of our Lord and Savior's heritage and ethnicity became hidden from His followers. All of the beauty of God's promises found in His feasts and celebrations; even prophetic events that have been fulfilled based on the Jewish calendar, were all hidden, snuffed out. Instead, new man-made rules and regulations (loosely based on Scripture) were put in place to benefit those in power, bolster the economy, and keep the people in order.

But God's plan is unstoppable! Repentance is all about turning around. No more cow paths and dead ends for us. We are turning onto God's "highway" and traveling toward an age-old epic quest. This era, the time of the Gentiles[2] (today's non-Jewish Christians) is giving way to the time of the Jews. The Jewish nation is comprehending Jesus as the Anointed One, their long-awaited

---

[2] Luke 21:24

CHAPTER 3: Why Do We Do This Again?

Messiah, more now than ever before. The Messianic Jews are growing in historic numbers each day. The Gentile-believers are beginning to discover their Jewish roots and embracing their heritage. God's plan of "one new humanity" is coming together before our very eyes. The Kingdom of God is still being established on earth by a surrendered people responding to God's mercy and grace with their whole hearts and very lives.

Seeing it for what it really is, exploring what it was meant to be, and being brave enough to wonder where this road goes, could help us on our way to the best destination ever! Throw out the old Sunday Afternoon Adventurer's Handbook and don't be afraid to turn around.

Will I still go on vacation this year? Probably. Will I console myself with pints of my favorite ice cream right out of the container while I'm there? It wouldn't be vacation if I didn't. Will I need a vacation when I get back? I might. But focusing on what I've loved about it in the past and remembering the mountaintop views and sweet moments I've already had may just open me up to the option of having a "staycation" avoiding all the annoyances and taking day trips instead.

Instead of looking for a change of scene,
maybe all we really need is a change of "seeing."

CHAPTER 4: Are We There Yet?

We may not say it out loud anymore, but I can bet you we all still think it. Only two blocks from where we've started, with 100 miles ahead of us, and you hear (either from an actual child in the back seat or from that inner child whining in your head): Are we there yet? We want to close our eyes, make a wish, and open them to see that we've been magically transported to our destination without the bother of traveling the miles to get there.

Just the thought of a long journey makes me want to stop before I start. I can talk myself out of any adventure simply by envisioning the drive, imagining the traffic, and dreading the distance or weather conditions. As you can tell, I am not someone who enjoys driving. I was 28 years old when I finally got my driver's license (out of absolute

CHAPTER 4: Are We There Yet?

necessity) and 32 years later, I still only drive when absolutely necessary. It's the process. The distance. The waiting. Ugh!

Telling me to get in the car and drive without the promise of a beautiful scenic destination (along with a motivational bag of sweet and salty bribery) is pretty much a trip to the gallows for me. Telling me to write a book about a church on wagon wheels without letting me know where it's headed falls into pretty much the same category. I guess if we were in a car right now, this chapter is right about where I'd be sighing heavily and whining loudly, "Are we there yet?" So, I think a little bribery is in order. If we can't know the destination, we should at least be able to snack on something yummy along the way!

Okay, so here's a little snacky something that caught my attention. God's concept of one new humanity, that came to light as I wrote the last chapter, felt sweetly significant to me somehow. I know *all* of His Word is extremely significant, but as far as where the church on wheels might be headed, this idea of being united in Christ Jesus, one people, under God, indivisible (hey, it's sounding vaguely familiar) feels like it could be an important part of our custom designed "direction package."

Having unity, oneness, unison, or community all require one thing. Actually, they require at least two. You need to have at least two people who agree or come together to achieve any of them. And, it would make sense that they would need to gather on a regular basis to experience the full impact.

Be on Your Way

I took a small survey of family and friends who have been to church and asked them what part they liked most about it, now or as a kid. Was there *anything* they remembered liking? The two common responses I got were: singing together (labeled as worship), and being with like-minded people (to which they all added, "You know, fellowship"). I have noticed I rarely hear the word fellowship used outside the context of talking about church. Though to me, fellowship seems much deeper than just thinking alike. I actually like seeking fellowship with people who think and see things differently. It can make experiencing life together so much more interesting — iron sharpening iron. Part of me wanted to change the answer to being with "like-hearted" people. As I wrestled with possibly misquoting people to fit more with my opinion, I realized that their description actually better reflected something the apostle Paul wrote. We are told to renew our minds,[3] to have the mind of Christ, and to adopt His attitude. In doing so we become united:

> Therefore, if you have any encouragement from being united with Christ, any comfort from his love, if any common sharing in the Spirit, if any tenderness and compassion, then make my joy complete by being like-minded, having the same love, being one in spirit and of one mind ... In your relationships with one another have the same mindset as Christ Jesus... (Philippians 2:1-2,5).

The phrase "having the same love" means each of us having our heart in tune with the Father's Heart, making us one in Spirit — each

---

[3] Romans 12:2

CHAPTER 4: Are We There Yet?

of us completely unique but completely united. Imagine what kind of impact a community of people like that could have! Don't you think that being of one heart and mind as a truly unified, compatible fellowship of loving people could completely change the world?

The other common response to my survey also got me thinking about how very rare it is in our culture to sing together as a group. Other than community performance groups and the occasional singing of *Happy Birthday*, most of us don't sing together in public except for maybe church or possibly at a baseball stadium during the seventh inning stretch. Would you agree that when we do chime in, it seems to assuage in us that across-the-board desire to be part of something bigger?

To do something in one accord can prove very satisfying. Consider the way it feels to cheer or chant at a game, to do things like the wave, or line dance at a wedding. Even applauding as an audience feels better than being that embarrassed solo clapper. Better yet, think of how fortifying the force behind clapping can be when the audience synchronizes each clap or stomp on the same beat. There's beauty in harmony, yes. But there is power in unison.

A drum and bugle corps can literally make your heart thump. A line of drummers beating intricate patterns with perfectly synchronized precision has the potential to electrify the atmosphere and resonate with the heart of the whole audience at once. But it's not just the beat. There is something mesmerizing about synchronized movement: schools of fish, flocks of birds, a flash mob of dancers. Two or three people all gracefully moving together is impressive, but a mass of people moving in rehearsed precision can be inspiring.

Do you think maybe God wired us to want to move in harmony like a school of fish, but created us to be able to *choose* to move together, and not to have to do it by mere instinct? The dramatic dancers' grand-finale kick line, or when a cast of people on stage all start moving forward in rehearsed, matching steps, inspires applause every time. It's obvious that it's not something that just happened; it took hours of work, and something inside of us recognizes that. But something else deep within us resonates with the beauty and power of so many unique individuals acting and moving as one ... by choice.

It's obvious that doing something in unison takes some kind of direction or prompting by a signal, beat, or cue of some sort, so when the illusion is created that the synchronization was spontaneous, we can't help but smile. Do you remember discovering the fun of sitting lined up side-by-side on a bench or a couch with friends, your legs crossed all in the same direction, and then at someone's discreet signal you would all uncross and then re-cross your legs going the other way? (If you have no idea what I'm talking about, do yourself a favor and get a bunch of friends together right now and try it.) Maybe we were just easily amused, but there was something so fun about an ordinary movement being "unexpectedly" done in unison in public. People noticing us would laugh every time. With a bit of practice and skillful execution, we could pull this off without observers knowing who the leader was, even though they knew of course there had to be one.

CHAPTER 4: Are We There Yet?

Two people might coincidentally move or say something at the same time. But 3, or 10, or 100? We instinctively know that it had to have been planned. The larger the group, the more likely it's practiced over and over for hours to make it happen impressively. For a group to be perfectly in sync without a plan or any rehearsal would have to be supernatural. And even then, it would still take a Leader.

A good leader overseeing a group of people all working together on a project, or trying to accomplish something important as a team, is hard to identify by casual observation. They're usually working side by side, sleeves rolled up, discreetly leading by example, sensitive to the team's strengths and weaknesses, and open to listening to their opinions and creative ideas.

> Jesus called them together and said, "You know that those who are regarded as rulers of the Gentiles lord it over them, and their high officials exercise authority over them. Not so with you. Instead, whoever wants to become great among you must be your servant, and whoever wants to be first must be slave of all. For even the Son of Man did not come to be served, but to serve, and to give His life as a ransom for many" (Mark 10:42-45).

> "I no longer call you servants, because a servant does not know his master's business. Instead, I have called you friends, for everything that I learned from my Father I have made known to you. You did not choose me, but I chose you and appointed you so that you might go and bear fruit — fruit that will last. Then the Father will

give you whatever you ask in My Name. This is My command: love each other." (John 15:15-17).

So, that's what church leaders are supposed to look like? If done the way Jesus instructed us, it would probably be hard to tell at a casual glance exactly who the leader of a group of congregants is. Up to this point in my church experiences, most times the congregation takes their cue from a person up front, or from sheer repetition (even then I think most of us look to a person sitting in front of us to take our cue from). "Let's stand and sing…" "Let us pray: Our Father…" "You may be seated." But the hardest one for me to oblige with is "Let's give the Lord a great big handclap!" Really? Has it come to that? Instructing me how and when to clap? Where is that in a leader's job description?

Have you ever been applauding at the end of a mediocre performance, maybe at a community theater or even a professional concert, where a few people in the front row are moved to give a standing ovation, and then out of politeness the rest of the audience feels obligated and straggles in clusters to their feet? And you, not at all impressed by the performance, figure, "Well I have to put my coat on anyhow, we're leaving, so I might as well stand up with the rest of them." Right, now compare that experience with a time you were with an audience or group of people at an event where something was done or said that was so moving the entire group responded in an outburst of approval, jumping to their feet in unison and appreciation, because there was no other option. No one could remain silent or indifferent.

CHAPTER 4: Are We There Yet?

I was worshiping with a small group of Christians one night. As the anointed musician continued to play his guitar after the lyrics were done, we all started singing praises in our own words or prayer language, some harmonizing, some making a joyful noise, but totally led and united by the Holy Spirit. That lasted for about five minutes and then the same way it had spontaneously started, it gently faded into a weighty and reverent silence. No one wanted to move or make a sound. We could feel the thick holiness of God's Presence. Then all at once, everyone burst into applause, some laughing, some crying, without any prompting needed. We were in one accord with each other because at that moment our hearts were in unison with the Father's.

If we could go back to God's original blueprint — before His instructions, gifts of the Spirit, and our rich Jewish heritage got tucked away on us — I'm pretty sure that unity, oneness, unison, and community would be a lot more evident in our gatherings. We wouldn't have to rely so much on our traditions, repetitions, and so-called Order of Service. "Moving as One" would come as we paid close attention to the cues and directions of the ultimate Leader, the Holy Spirit. The more closely we'd each follow His lead, moving to His rhythm, the more in sync we would become with each other. But it would mean all of us acknowledging our need for Him and being open to His supernatural directing. Can you imagine how special that would be to Jesus and what that would mean to our Heavenly Father to see us all in sync?

Be on Your Way

How good and pleasant it is when brothers live together in unity! It is like precious oil poured on the head, running down on the beard, running down on Aaron's beard, down upon the collar of his robe (Psalm 133:1-2).

Aaron was the first priest appointed as a mediator between the Israelites and God, but only as a foreshadow of God's One true Mediator to come — Messiah Jesus. The fragrant anointing oil poured over Aaron's head onto his priestly robes was God's picture of His Holy Spirit bringing His children into perfect unity of spirit and mind.

Jesus' ultimate desire for us is seen clearly as He prays for us the night before He was tortured and crucified:

> My prayer is not for them [the disciples] alone. I pray also for those who will believe in me through their message, that all of them may be one, Father, just as you are in me and I am in you. May they also be in us so that the world may believe that you have sent me. I have given them the glory that you gave me, that they may be one as we are one: I in them and you in me. May they be brought to complete unity to let the world know that you sent me and have loved them even as you have loved me (John 17:20-23).

The sweetness of Jesus Himself praying to the Father that we would be brought into complete unity with Him, and with each other, is enough to keep me hopeful. World peace is not just a beauty contestant's perfect answer to what they most desire. It's Jesus' heart's cry and the Father's perfect plan. What leaves me dumbfounded is

CHAPTER 4: Are We There Yet?

that He needs our cooperation to achieve it. We are not puppets or forced laborers. We are His children — stubborn children — but *His* nonetheless. He knows each of us intimately. He loves us despite our foolishness and stubborn wills and will not abandon or leave us behind at the next rest stop even if we've been whining since we left the driveway. Nor will He force us to get back in the car. But this bit of sweet bribery, seeing a glimpse of His heart, has made me want to keep writing in hopes of seeing where He's taking us.

Are we there yet? Obviously not. But we're getting that much closer.

Here ... have another chocolate-covered pretzel.

CHAPTER 5: How About We Sing a Song?

Waiting! Waiting at a long red light when you're late for work. Waiting at the drive-through at lunchtime when you skipped breakfast that day because you were late for work. Waiting in line at the DMV (to renew your expiring driver's license) when your lunch break is almost over because the fast-food drive-through took so long. Waiting for the big hand to hit the 12 so you can get home to feed the cat that you just remembered you forgot to feed that morning because you were running late. Waiting in the bumper-to-bumper 5:00 traffic jam just hoping that your favorite chair will be spared from the hunger-crazed cat claws that for sure shredded the rest of the house. Waiting at the walk-in clinic to have said cat surgically removed from your hand because the cat food cupboard was bare when you finally did get home.

CHAPTER 5: How About We Sing a Song?

Whether you're waiting with excited anticipation or with fearful dread, waiting is hard work for all of us. I don't think I can name one person, young or old, who enjoys waiting. Fred Rogers had a great song that addressed the issue and suggested that we "think of something to do while we're waiting, while we're waiting for something new to do." The man was brilliant, but I think you'll agree that keeping distracted only helps for so long. Still, it's worth a shot.

Traveling long distances is all about waiting to get there. Hence, alphabet games ("A" my name is Alice), license plate games, travel bingo, padiddle, punch buggy, and whatever else you have come up with along the way; listening to audio books, music, or a live sporting event (till you drive out of range and miss the final score); anything we can find to do to distract us from the "foreverness" of the wait. At times we even get desperate enough to sing songs, even countdown songs about bottles on a wall, or songs that never end (yes, they go on and on, my friend). I think it's been scientifically proven that they make whoever's driving drive all that much faster.

But what do we do when we're waiting for a promise from God: that something good is coming our way, that He is going to rescue us out of our difficult circumstances, or heal us as promised by His Name, Jehovah Rapha (the God Who Heals)? How do we keep our hopes up when it's been years and years of waiting? How do we combat insidious unbelief and doubt that creep into our once hopeful heart because nothing appears to be changing? What game or song can distract us from that without driving us crazy?

Be on Your Way

Then it struck me: What if, as I cry out: "How long O Lord? How much longer are You going to make me wait?" what if He has actually been waiting all this time for *me* to do something. He's given me an idea, or direction, and I've been too afraid to run with it or swing the racket. He's already served me the ball and it's been in my court this whole time. I've been sitting here twirling the racket thinking I'm being so patient, when He's the One who's patiently waiting on me to take a swing.

Many of us have been navigating through life by looking ahead to the next big event to keep our minds off of the present challenges. In grade school we look forward to middle school, in middle school to high school, and in high school we just want to graduate so we can finally be treated like adults and go to college, where it becomes all about GPA's, graduating, careers, promotions and raises. For some, first comes love, then comes marriage, then comes shopping for a baby carriage (so we can then look forward to the big events in our children's lives as well) because that's what we've learned to do to keep ourselves motivated. We keep looking ahead. Everyone's life is not always in the same order. We may not all have common goals or experience the same life events, but we all share in that same looking forward to what's next to motivate us onward, or at least to get us up in the morning.

As life goes along, we find out that the future is unpredictable and not always what we had in mind. Even if we think something is inevitable, we find out along the way that you can't count your

CHAPTER 5: How About We Sing a Song?

chickens, and unfortunately, you can't always count on people. Looking ahead becomes more like dread. Fear of the future is obviously a common fear for many, proven by the number of fortunetellers and psychics who are raking in … well, a "fortune." Even crowds of Christians (who know spiritists and mediums are off limits) are instead lining up to get a free, personal "prophetic word" from well-known Christian prophets. It's a fine line between listening for God, trusting Him to help us make wise choices, and seeking out someone who hears from Him to tell us what He says (often so we don't have to do the work or take sole responsibility if things go wrong).

There are many of us who fear the unknown and want to have our futures made clear to us, hoping for a guaranteed outcome and a reason not to worry. Fears of making wrong decisions, of embarrassment, and of disappointment also play into our desire of having someone else tell us what to do. But God's promises and prophetic words are not provided to forecast our future like a fortune cookie — will I get the job, will I be married soon, should I, or shouldn't I go? Prophetic words and Scriptural promises are given to us to hold on to, and fight with when doubt and resistance meet us as we pursue God's call on our lives.

Of course, encouraging words prayed and declared over us make us feel affirmed and loved; they may confirm words God has previously brought to our attention, but that by no means gives us permission to just sit back and wait for things to happen. God programmed us to move, to take action, to reach out, and to follow His lead. Promises and prophecies are meant to move us forward, to inspire us to take action.

The way we're designed to fulfill our destiny while squeezing the most fun out of getting there is to know, grow, and learn more from our Heavenly Dad by watching what He's doing and then joining in. Sometimes we see Him holding up that one-more-minute finger, with a slight smirk on His face. It's hard for us to accept the fact that God would actually tell us to wait when He knows how much "I want it now!" And even worse, we can't believe that He could possibly be telling us we're not quite ready, stay where we are and try it again. Are You kidding; go over it one more time? I don't want to have to practice musical scales again and again in order to be able to play the masterpiece He has written just for me to play. I want to play it *now!*

So much of how we learn is to repeat an action or thought over and over until our muscles or mind learn the pattern. Learning to walk, talk, ride a bike, play an instrument, wink, whistle, bat a baseball — all by repetition of movement. Remember learning whatever it was by someone guiding your hand, or moving you in the necessary direction to accomplish it? We train ourselves by repeating the action. Eventually we do whatever it is simply by memory without thinking about it. In fact, if we think about it too much, we struggle with what we're trying to do. For most of us, if we try describing to someone step by step how we're managing to walk across the room — if we really focus on how we're shifting our balance, which muscles we're

CHAPTER 5: How About We Sing a Song?

using, which part of our foot feels the most pressure at which point in the motion forward — it gets really complicated. Are we leaning towards or away from the foot that's moving, and what's with our arms at that moment? Are they swinging? Are wrists upturned or straight down? Do feet turn slightly out, or in, or straight ahead? If you think too much, you can stand there for hours paralyzed or possibly end up tripping over your own feet.

We're actually capable of doing things way beyond our skill set just by practicing ... a lot. I would not consider myself a pianist. I can read notes one at a time, but not the chords or bass clef quickly enough to play piano music. But because of hours spent as a teenager deciphering chords note by note, and sheer repetition, I can still play the introduction to Handel's *Hallelujah Chorus* on the piano simply by finger memory. If I think about what I'm doing even a little, I can't get past the first two chords. I can't even tell you what those chords are right now. My fingers just know where my hands need to be when I sit down at a piano.

Sometimes our brains actually need our body memories to recall information. An action, pattern, or melody by which we learned something triggers our brain memory. I still sing (in my head) part of the alphabet song when looking up a word in the dictionary. I use hand-motions to remember Bible verses, and actions on stage to cue my brain to recall some of my hard to remember lines in a play.

It feels like I just took us on an unnecessary detour and I'm having a hard time finding the way back to the highway. Let's pull over and look at the scenery for a minute while we wait and see if the main idea comes back in view. Sometimes that's all it takes: changing our focus, retracing our steps. What turn got us here? Just give it a minute. So much has happened in the spiritual realm since I first heard the title of this book a few months ago. I've been waiting and waiting to see what comes next, writing it down and then listening and watching for more. But I feel like God is moving so fast that by the time I publish this, it will be old news. And yet here I wait day by day, pencil in hand, listening, questioning, "Was that really you, God?" Then He makes sure prophetic voices from around the world are speaking back to me, confirming within a day or two what I thought I heard Him say. I'm not the only one feeling His prompting, feeling that there is an urgency behind this book being completed and distributed to His people, but unable to finish it without waiting to hear His voice. His timing is perfect. And there is character-building happening, lessons of faith, learning to trust in the waiting.

Waiting on God is not meant to make us all antsy, confused, and frustrated. It should renew our strength to soar above circumstances on wings as eagles.[4] In other words, putting our hope in God's goodness and trusting that His plan for us is best (even if we don't know what it is yet) should encourage us to look up and anticipate sweet surprises ahead. When our thinking or circumstances have overwhelmed us, and we start to doubt the sweetness of the surprise, singing to Him, worshiping Him, reading His Love Letters (the Bible)

---

[4] See Isaiah 40:31

CHAPTER 5: How About We Sing a Song?

and remembering His faithfulness can almost work like body-memory. It overrides our thoughts and draws us up above the doubt and uncertainty.

We've all been surrounded at one time or another by unwelcome circumstances. They may not be our fault, though sometimes they are. Even so, however we got there, chances are the way out can seem elusive to us in the moment. We cry out for a hand to rescue us, and when most pass us by on the other side of the road, we start questioning who our real friends and neighbors truly are. Then we usually move on to questioning God's love for us, His fairness, or our worthiness. It's hard for me to believe that there are times when being stranded right where I am can be for my benefit. Being delayed could actually protect me from arriving someplace too soon, before I'm ready. Being unprepared could be more harmful or dangerous for me than being detained.

I am not the only one waiting. It's helpful for me to know that I have not been singled out. I may be the only one waiting for things in *my* life to happen, but the truth is all of creation is waiting for us, the sons and daughters of God, to be revealed[5] and for the return of King Jesus.

After a lifetime in the car, if we think we're almost there and we find out that we have hours to go, we can become so deflated that every minute that passes becomes even more torturous. Just before

---

[5] Romans 8:19

Be on Your Way

Jesus returned to heaven, and His disciples asked what would be the sign of His coming into power and of the end of the age, He described what the world would be like before He returned to Jerusalem for good, to reign over all the nations — His Kingdom without end. His disciples pressed Him to find out when exactly that would be. Jesus implied that they didn't need to know that right now. It's similar to the prophet Daniel (after asking for revelation of what all the visions God showed him meant) being told by God to seal up his prophetic book, it was not for Daniel to know. It would be revealed instead to those in the last of the last days who really needed to know. Only then would they be able to put it all together.

Can you imagine how discouraging it would have been for Jesus to tell His followers, "Sorry guys, you're not going to see Me again here on earth in your lifetime"? It was so much kinder for Jesus to leave possibilities open for every generation. He encourages us to live life at the ready, as if He was returning any minute. That's how we endure the waiting period — by living every minute to the fullest.

Instead of wallowing in the mud, whining, "How long O Lord?" look for a way out. It may not be an escalator or an elevator. It will probably take more than pressing a button. It could be an old splintery ladder or a frayed rope that needs climbing. If there's none to be seen and no one nearby to assist you, think of something to do while you're waiting. Try making mud pies, or give yourself a mud-mask facial, add straw and make bricks, play a game, sing a song, but never lose sight of the possibility that any day could be *the* day. Trusting in God's

CHAPTER 5: How About We Sing a Song?

goodness and faithfulness, recalling all the times before He has redeemed us from muddy pits and crowned us with love and compassion, makes the waiting not only bearable, but beneficial and practical. It's basic training. It's learning and practicing the motions until they become so much a part of us, we'll know what to do in the future without having to think about it.

If you've been calling out for help for what seems like years, and you find yourself still waiting to be rescued, ask yourself a few questions: Is there something I'm supposed to be doing to get *myself* out of here? Have I had the ruby slippers all this time? Am I not trying because I'm afraid of failing? Are my circumstances all I can handle right now? Would that promotion, or that marriage proposal, that new house, ministry, or family inheritance, be more than I could physically or emotionally sustain? Would I collapse under the weight of the responsibility of it? Would it be more of a curse for me then this muddy rut I seem to be stuck in presently? It sure feels like anything would be better than this torturously long, bumpy ride-of-a-life that I'm enduring.

Hey, didn't we just pass that sign an hour ago? Is it time for the alphabet game? Wait I have a great idea!

How about we sing a song? I know just the one.

CHAPTER 6: Which Way is Up?

The "wonder where this road goes" game was most fun for me when I was with someone who had a good sense of direction and a pretty good idea of where we actually might be. Being disoriented for a moment can be fun, like on an amusement park ride, or while trying to find the backside of a paper donkey after being blindfolded and spun holding the sticky-tape attached to its tail. More than a minute of disorientation, however, and it's not exactly enjoyable anymore.

Then there are those unexpected silly moments of feeling totally turned around. Have you ever gotten off the elevator on the wrong floor and taken a few steps down the hall before you realize you're not where you thought you were? Right building, wrong floor. It's a bit embarrassing and you hope the doors to the elevator are still open so you can slip back in unnoticed. If not, you pretend you got off on

CHAPTER 6: Which Way is Up?

purpose to find the stairs and climb up two flights to the actual intended floor for ... uh ... the exercise, yeah, that's it, the exercise.

What about trying to open up the wrong car in the crowded parking lot, wondering whose strange sunglasses got left on the console and why isn't your key working? It doesn't take long to figure out the mistake and as long as nobody notices, we usually laugh it off. I'm curious though: If you don't *know* that you're lost, are you still lost? Or are you only lost the moment you realize you're not where you thought you were? And if a tree falls in the woods and you're not there to hear it (because you're lost) does it make a sound? Does anybody know? Does anybody care? Probably not. But we do know that if a person is lost in the woods without a compass or reference point, they tend to walk in circles. Which circles me back to my original question: Do you think we're lost? Have we, as the Church, lost our way?

Part of *not* being lost is knowing where you are in relation to where you started, or at least knowing in which direction your destination lies. Do we even remember where we started? Have we been making any progress, or are we still going around the mountain one more time? When walking or running on a track, your destination, or goal, becomes how fast or how many times you can complete a lap. Does each time around make us stronger or just dizzier? Does that describe the Church? Other than doing laps on a track, going in circles indicates we're probably lost or confused.

Maybe that's where God is taking us in this chapter: to a place where we can see the possibility that we may not actually be where we think we are. We may even have to be willing to ask for help.

Ah, the infamous struggle of having to stop and ask for directions. We thought it was a thing of the past as soon as our cars and cellphones started coming with built-in navigation systems. For most people it felt like it happened overnight, but for some of us "not born yesterday," there was a learning curve and a lot of stumbling our way through the ever-advancing navigational technology.

First, we had to figure out how to fold up those impossible to refold paper maps. They really should have included directions on how to fold the directions. Then technically challenged individuals such as myself had to master printing out convenient online directions to take along, which I eventually did after being painstakingly led through the process by our then 10-year-old daughter a few times. Next came the screen mounted to your dashboard that led you along the way with a creepy moving map that disconcertingly knew exactly where you were. As long as you had an extra half hour to figure out how to select the right icons to get to where you were going, and then were able to decipher the upside-down screen that inevitably dismounted its way to the passenger-side floor, you could get at least halfway to your destination before having to pull over and unfold the old crumpled up paper map stuffed in the glove compartment. The challenge became not so much following directions, but doing so

CHAPTER 6: Which Way is Up?

without driving into ditches or oncoming traffic in the process. It was novel and very high tech, so we plowed through.

And here we are now, with phones and cars that come pre-equipped to meet our every directional need at the sound of a voice command. No glitches or ditches. That is until ... [reverb, please, for dramatic effect]: the dead zone. You've been tootling along and your little navigating friend has been gently directing you at every "right, left, and continue straight" even though you haven't needed her because you've driven this particular part of the trip a thousand times. But here it comes — the left-hand turn that takes you into unfamiliar territory. You've entered a labyrinth of quaintly-named lanes and terraces, a network of twists and turns that would confuse even a professional laboratory mouse. You're grinning to yourself thinking, "No problem, I've got me my navigating expert." All of a sudden, for no apparent reason as you approach the stop sign expecting the next friendly directive command, everything falls dead silent. You look down to see the map frozen at the last turn. There you sit paralyzed, still a couple miles from your destination, not sure if you could even begin to remember how to backtrack through the maze you just came through. Neighbors are walking by wondering why you've parked at their stop sign, and now there's a car behind you. The inside of your vehicle is getting stuffy and smaller, or so it seems, as the onlookers stare and the impatient honking begins. There's only one obvious thing to do: roll your window down and ... get some fresh air riding around till you get the signal back, right? Anything but asking for directions.

Be on Your Way

Why are we so quick to listen to an impersonal satellite voice and follow "her" directions, but we won't roll down our window and ask a person who obviously lives nearby how to get back on track? Who are we trying to impress?

It would only make sense that Jesus would tell those of us feeling like "we got this," that the way we become great in the Kingdom of Heaven, the way we get on track, is to become like a little child[6] and to admit, "I guess, we don't got this." We need to be willing to receive from the King all the treasures He wants to show us. He wants to share everything He has stored up for us. All we have to do is stop saying "I can do this myself" and ask Him for directions.

Have you ever watched as someone struggles with something because they're too close to it and can't see the whole picture? From your angle you can see exactly what the problem is. But they refuse to listen to you. "No thanks, I got this." How many times a day do we say that to God? It's like we're trying to convince Him that we really know what we're doing, while trying to convince ourselves at the same time. We are quicker to believe and take directions off the internet than from our personal Advisor who literally has a God's-eye view.

I had a refrigerator magnet for the longest time that said "Better ask your teenagers now while they still know everything." Even after my kids had grown, I kept it to remind me of my own prideful tendency. Maybe it just comes from years of having to know the right

---

[6] See Matthew 18:2-4

CHAPTER 6: Which Way is Up?

answer on tests and spelling bees, or having to know vital information on the spot as a mom with active kids who often threw caution to the wind, then later in life as a caregiver of elderly parents, having to know life and death information at the drop of a hat. And not just the fashion, homework, or relationship crisis solutions, but critical information too, like allergies, sensitivities, and entire medical histories. I had to be able to accurately fill in the ambulance driver or emergency room attendant while so much adrenaline was pumping that my teeth would be chattering. Filling out new-patient forms became anxiety causing. At this point in time, I don't need to know everybody else's information anymore, but it's all still in my head, and I can't remember whose medical history belongs to whom or which one is actually mine; they've all blended together. It's embarrassing. It's one reason I avoid switching doctors.

When God is repositioning us and planting us in new places or circumstances that are so beyond our capabilities it feels like we're in way over our heads, previously vital information is no longer helpful and can make us confused. We feel disoriented. Not just the wrong floor this time, more like the wrong building. But I don't think we're completely lost or as off course as it feels. It's more like that anecdote about the old New England farmer giving directions to a tourist: after starting to point one way, stopping himself and then changing and pointing in the opposite direction, stopping and starting his verbal instructions a few different times, and then pointing back to the original direction, he finally scratches his head coming to the conclusion that "you can't get thaya from heeya." It may feel like we can't, but God is the God of the impossible. He loves to make a way where there is no way. I don't think we're completely lost, but I don't think we're understanding just how far away from God's original intention we have strayed.

Institutions are so foundational and well-organized that they seem like something God would intend for us, wouldn't you agree? When did God's original call to "one new humanity united by love" jump over to being a man-made religious institution described by many critics as a bunch of power-hungry, money-making hypocrites? Sadly, to some extent they are right. When did we lose our way?

When an organization is self-formed for charitable reasons, even those with altruistic intent can inadvertently morph from relational to institutional without much effort. Well-received at first, as the numbers and donations increase, intended beneficiaries start having to serve the system or institution by jumping through hoops, meeting certain criteria, and following strictly enforced regulations. The number of eligible recipients gets weeded out and allows funds to be reallocated. And practically overnight, the "charitable" founders of the institutions (i.e. hospitals, universities, diocese, etc.) suddenly become the ones who are benefiting the most.

When our offerings are lining pockets and not giving aid to those who we thought were the recipients, we start labeling any charity looking for donations as self-serving. We may not say it aloud but we think to ourselves: *They're probably all just scam artists taking advantage of good-hearted, generous people.* We get skeptical, and rightly so.

CHAPTER 6: Which Way is Up?

It's funny that most of us don't believe a self-formed commercial enterprise trying to tug on our heart strings through manipulative advertising is doing anything wrong. Most commercials are designed to change society's behavior and habits solely to make money. They blatantly present falsehoods, appealing to our need to be accepted, and instilling fear with slogans like "Dandruff will make you friendless," or "You'll be fired if you wear the wrong lip-shade," yet we don't condemn them for it. We actually support them by buying their products, especially if their commercial makes us vulnerable to manipulation by playing on our emotions with something touching or funny. We don't label businesses or manufacturers as hypocritical institutions or evil scams, even though in an attempt to convince you to buy their product, some companies claim to donate partial proceeds to worthy causes. That way you're not just saving your reputation by using their products, you're helping save the world by buying them.

The very fact God describes the Church as His Body, His Bride, makes us much more organic than organizational: God-appointed, God-designed, God-governed, God-chosen. As soon as a group of people segments itself into self-governing, self-appointed, self-organized, tax-exempt and a charitable organization under the banner of God-ordained, an institutional offspring is born and a skeptical eyebrow is raised by those watching. The organic paper map gets crumpled into the glove box and abstract technology gives us a false sense of knowing where we are. To where exactly has Institution Road led us?

Be on Your Way

In an evangelical circle of Christians (who are *truly* trying to save the world), you'll often hear the phrase: *Christianity is not about a religion, it's about a relationship.* And I agree. If we define "religion" as our effort to attain right-standing and favor with a deity (or possibly, as some see it, our self-effort to achieve spiritual awareness reaching an alternate, higher, state of being), then how can the *religion* of Christianity be about a relationship? It's all about God rescuing us from that impossible religious task of exhausting self-effort, and instead, personally bringing those of us who let Him, into an awareness of His presence and His perfect, unconditional, restorative love through Jesus. Spirit and body, faith and tangible evidence, collide in the Blood of Jesus, and a relationship is born. Our Rescuer's strong, loving hand can be experienced here and now, as we encounter His overwhelming peace, and see supernatural healings and happenings with our own eyes — that's Christianity.

Now along that same line of thinking, when we talk about Institutional Church vs. Relational Church, we're simply saying God is trying to move His Church (one new humanity, Jew and Gentile) back into a relational, loving, self-sacrificing way of life. We're being snatched up and out of an institutional, corporate-ladder, bottom-line-get-to-heaven paradigm. We have been created for way more than being a corporation of "do-gooders" just trying to outdo the competition by winning over more clients and growing our numbers. The fact that people attend our gatherings has nothing to do with success or victory. Rather, are we carrying out our Commander's mandate to not only preach the good news of forgiveness and

CHAPTER 6: Which Way is Up?

reconciliation with God, but what about: raising the dead, healing the sick, cleansing the lepers, and casting out demons? Are we loving God with our whole being and loving our neighbors as ourselves? [7]

Our collective job description, and the purpose of the Church, is to pray and declare God's Kingdom come and His will to be done on earth as it is in heaven. We are here to take back Kingdom territory, including releasing captives who are held in emotional, physical, and spiritual bondage. God gives us everything we need — our gifts, our talents, our resources, everything — to take back all the enemy has stolen from us. We have the authority to advance and reclaim. God doesn't want us backed into a corner, our shields of faith protecting us from the evil attacks and attempts of the devil. That only keeps us tucked out of the way in fear. God is trying to help us understand our authority and mandate to overwhelm the gates of hell, not by the institution of religion, but by relationally loving one another and sacrificially loving the broken and hard-to-love people we are surrounded with on a daily basis. We are to love them with our time, patient endurance, financial support, and words of encouragement. We don't have to look for them, or travel to some unheard-of place to find them. He brings them to us wherever we are, wherever we go.

When some critics of Christianity hear that we are instructed to especially love and sacrifice for others in the Body of Christ, it may sound to them as if we're just another exclusive club, bigoted and self-serving. But part of our God-given requirements for living

---

[7] Matthew 10:8 & 22:37

Be on Your Way

as a follower of Jesus is to love our neighbors as ourselves, consider them first, but even beyond that, we're instructed by Jesus to love not just our friends, but to love our enemies; and not just say we love them, or try to feel love for them, but to show our love for them with actions and words of blessing.[8] That would be the opposite of bigoted and exclusive, wouldn't you say?

Taking special care of brothers and sisters in Christ, fellow warriors in the battle against dark, malicious spiritual entities, is like M.A.S.H. units focusing on wounded soldiers, or U.S.O. Tours trying to encourage and build up the troops. They're designed to help the enlisted personnel. It's not saying that civilians can't enlist or that they're not just as important to God as those who are already enlisted. We are all loved, unique, and born on purpose. It's just that the supernatural gifts given to Spirit-filled believers to minister to one another are given with God's ultimate goal that an edified, healthy Church will in turn be effective, loving, ministers enabled to reach out to everyone — especially every civilian — God puts in their path. And aren't soldiers actually fighting for the lives of loved-ones, family, and nation?

How do we find our way from institutional back to relational? It starts with admitting we may be off track or going around the same track out of habit. We are each a part of the Body, and every cell has its job to do. We each need to listen for our individual God-given directions and strategies and be quick to obey Him. Sometimes that

---

[8] Matthew 5:44

CHAPTER 6: Which Way is Up?

means stepping out by vulnerably expressing our hearts or offering to others something new God just showed us. It also means, we must be willing to open ourselves up to humbly hear what others have to share — believing that God has been instructing them as well. Our position, status, rank or letters that come or don't come after our names, make no difference to God, so why should they matter to us? He gives wisdom freely to all who ask. And He often uses the foolish to confound the wise. Great or small, because of Him, we *all* have experiences, insights, and a unique perspective that He intends us to share with others. We can learn so much more when we value each other enough to put ourselves out there, and be really good listeners.

Rolling down our metaphorical windows and asking for directions from real live people, possibly even strangers, humbly readies us to be redirected and repositioned by God's Positioning System: The Ultimate Navigator.

He knows exactly where we are, where we're headed, how to get us there, and in the end ... how to get us Home.

CHAPTER 7: How Far Can We Get on Fumes?

If you remember when gas station attendants came out to service your car by filling the tank, washing the windshield, checking the oil, and sending you on your way, you will probably be able to relate to my next observation. During these past 60 years of my life, my tastes have changed with what seems like the seasons. Now and again, you notice that what used to bring you satisfaction, even joy, no longer has the same luster, and things only your grandparents used to like suddenly look appealing. All along life's way, one minute you absolutely love certain music, décor, styles, entertainment, hobbies, and the next you're asking yourself, how could you have possibly? Tastes can change at any stage of life, but lately for us it's been a change in our literal taste — in food. Granted, we may still like the taste of something, but suddenly it doesn't like us. What we once could eat a dozen of now tastes better in bite-size portions. Combine that

CHAPTER 7: How Far Can We Get on Fumes?

with becoming more sensitive to certain flavors, and agreeing on a restaurant with someone else who's also experiencing a sophistication of their taste buds (as well as possible dietary restrictions) can make going out to eat a challenging game of skill, balance, and strategy:

"Last Restaurant Standing"

OBJECT OF THE GAME: Eating a meal that you won't regret.

BEGINNING THE GAME: The person who usually cooks the meal says, "I don't feel like cooking supper tonight." The other person accepts the challenge with, "Where do you want to go?"

ROUND 1: Each player names every place they *don't* want to go and lists all the possible annoyances that could be encountered there including but not limited to: wait time, noise level, service, grease and sodium content of the food, amount of typical spices used (including MSG), and unreasonable prices. "Not feeling like a certain category of food" is half valid and counts as half a point.

ROUND 2: Whoever wins Round 1 by ruling out the most restaurants with valid reasons can then challenge Player 2. THE CHALLENGE: Player 1 agrees to pay for supper if Player 2 can come up with even one possible remaining place within a 30-minute radius or whatever timeframe falls into the "avoiding-heartburn-window" of not eating after 6:30 PM.

ROUND 3: If Player 2 accepts and meets the challenge, said Player becomes the WINNER and is treated to supper by Player 1. If there

Be on Your Way

is no feasible restaurant left to name then Player 2 defaults and is then responsible for serving cereal for supper to both players without grumbling.

GAME OVER

When I'm really hungry, I will eat just about anywhere and even eat food that is not my favorite. Go to the grocery store hungry and what do you come home with? Our condition greatly influences our decisions. If I find myself driving some place in unfamiliar territory and I glance at the fuel tank to see that it's nearly full, I consider myself on an exploit and enjoy the trip. If there's a sign like the one at the start of a scenic New Hampshire highway that says, "No gas for the next 32 miles," I'll feel a twinge of anxiety even if I just filled the tank. But sign or no sign, when the gauge says "near empty" I become very disconcerted and my whole focus changes to finding the shortest route to the nearest gas station.

Right now, it feels like the Western Church has a broken gas gauge that is registering "near full" when it's actually almost empty and a no-gas-for-32-miles sign keeps flashing in my head. I keep getting the sense that my assignment, this book, is to tap on that gauge till it registers the truth that something is missing; that we need to feel the hunger pangs again because it's imperative for all of us to want to fill up. We as the Bride of Christ must connect into the power God has ready for us. He's waiting near the fuel pump hoping we'll stop by so He can fill us up, clear our vision, and give us some fresh oil. But we need to be so hungry that we are ready for anything. No more indecision because we're not that hungry or we don't feel like eating at that particular moment. Our tastes may have changed in this season, but we need to be open to the next-level fuel God has for us.

Are we running on fumes? Have we been functioning on the success of the business-paradigm (covered with the scent of spirituality) for so long that we have forgotten what it feels like to operate by the powerful fuel of God's Holy Spirit, supernaturally driving His Church forward into enemy territory and overpowering the darkness with the actual Glory of God — being strong in the Lord and in the power of *His* might?[9] Are you seeing the illusion of spirituality most of us have been living under, the fumes we've been running on?

We hear over and over when visiting churches that they believe in the gifts of the Spirit but they're not operating in them. They know Christ is Healer, and that we can pray for healing. But most think that they need to pray "if it's Your will, God, to heal them, then please do it." When the reality of the power we carry within us, the same power of the Holy Spirit Who raised Jesus from the dead, says we will lay hands on the sick and they shall recover, isn't it obvious that it's God's will for us to command healing? We are given strict instructions by Jesus Himself (in Matthew 10:8) to cast out demons, heal the sick, raise the dead, and cleanse the leper. Yet we have made it into spiritually figurative commands to cast out the demon of worldly thinking, heal

---

[9] See Ephesians 6:10

the spiritually sick by preaching to them, raise the spiritually dead by getting them to see the error of their ways and pray a sinner's prayer, and spiritually cleanse the ostracized by bringing them back into community and getting them to go to church. I'm sorry to say I believed it for years and I have dear friends that still feel this way. The deception has tangled even very mature believers into what can be referred to as "unbelieving believers." Maybe that's you. Like the father of the boy in Mark 9:24 asking Jesus to heal his son said, "I do believe; help me overcome my unbelief!" Maybe you know what the Scriptures say but fear, doubt, or unbelief keep creeping into your thinking causing confusion or double-mindedness.

Recently, I had an odd experience while on vacation. We were watching TV one night in a condo we've stayed in for years, never seeing "nature" inside the place before. My husband suddenly said, "What is that?!" pointing to something crawling across the living room floor straight toward me. Granted, the shadow it cast made it appear larger, but it was big enough to be easily seen in just a TV lit room. Now, I don't mind spiders so much (I usually capture them and put them outside) but this guy was BIG, fast, and appeared to be on a malicious mission. Barefoot as I was, I grabbed a half empty box of tissue and after apologizing, "Sorry spider," I squashed it. Shortly thereafter, my husband went up to bed. As I continued watching the show, what appeared to be a mouse-like creature came out of nowhere and was scurrying right along the floor — the same travel-line as the previous invader — heading straight toward me. "What in the world?" It was not a mouse. I got a bit closer and saw the biggest, furriest

CHAPTER 7: How Far Can We Get on Fumes?

spider this side of the Amazon. I grabbed the tissue box yet again, and thought, "This is going to leave a stain." The first whack only stunned it. I think the spider actually laughed at me. The second try mostly stopped it, but it took me three times slamming that creature with a half-empty box of tissue to finally put it to rest. "Okay, that was weird." Dream interpreter that I am, if it had been a dream I would think, "Oh what a tangled web we weave…" And why a tissue box? I knew it had to do with deliverance and no matter how creepy something may look it only took a tissue box to get rid of it. Maybe it represented speaking a name seeming feather-weight to some, but the authority and power that the Name of Jesus carries can stop any force in its tracks. All right, but why three times for the stubborn big one?

About a month or so later, we were visiting a church and during the singing I walked across to the back row to get a Bible that I saw lying there. It was next to a tissue box. And guess what was also next to the box — Yep, the little jumpy kind. "God, what are you trying to tell me?" So I took the box and did what I do, but it jumped to the floor, out of commission but still moving. This time I had a shoe on. Then like Romans 16:20 says "The God of peace will soon crush satan under your feet." After the meeting, I was talking with two very prophetic women I had just met. I told them the story of the three spiders and the tissue boxes. Their observations were insightful. The conclusion we came to was that God has given me the ability to spot deception (Oh what a tangled web) especially in His Church, and has given me the tools to stomp it out by dealing with it at the emotional core (tissue box). Why three spiders? And why three times to take out the big one? God answered, "All you need is the Name, the Blood, and the Word."

Because of the Cross of Jesus, the only weapon satan has left is deception. The Truth of God's Word overrides the lie at the root of every fear, big or small. The Blood overcomes any power, and the Name carries all authority both in Heaven and on earth.

Maybe you're immersed in church-life, actively participating in ministry, maturing spiritually, gaining wisdom, and pouring into others' lives. You would describe yourself as thriving and content. God bless you and carry on! But maybe that describes you only up to a certain point because you're not content. You feel like something is missing, that there's something more. You sense God is calling you out of your familiar church surroundings, and you keep telling yourself it couldn't possibly be God. He wouldn't tell me to stop doing what I'm doing, the way I've been doing it. He wouldn't ask me to try and change anything so tried and true as our beloved traditions and programs. It may scare people away. He would never ask me to leave my church family and head off into unknown territory. There must be something wrong with me, or at least wrong with my spiritual ears. I should be content with where I am. You may even be rebuking the idea of being on your way. I know how you feel. I know it feels like an Abrahamic moment, but God is repositioning so many of His people. It's not a bad thing. It's not a falling away. It's a calling, a reassignment, and a reconfiguring of His troops. Instead of getting

CHAPTER 7: How Far Can We Get on Fumes?

trapped in sticky apprehension, listen to God speak His web-cutting truth:

> So do not fear, for I am with you; do not be dismayed, for I am your God. I will strengthen you and help you; I will uphold you with my righteous right hand. Have I not commanded you? Be strong and courageous. Do not be afraid; Do not be discouraged, for the Lord your God will be with you wherever you go. I will instruct you and teach you in the way you should go; I will counsel you with my loving eye on you. The Lord himself goes before you and will be with you; he will never leave you nor forsake you. Do not be afraid; do not be discouraged.[10]

Dear Reader, I so wish you could talk back to me right now so I could hear where you're coming from and what God is showing you. We have so much to learn from each other. God made us this way. He wants us to be open to each other's experiences and ideas, to be able to learn and grow together. God just reminded me of something I wrote down a few weeks ago. I thought it was just for me (even though He told me it was for the Church and not to leave a single word out no matter how absurd it sounded to me). See what you think:

> *Fear not. I am your God. You have a job to do and its description is encoded in your DNA. As you look to Me, read My Word, hear Me speak, you will activate the frequency code to unlock your destiny song. Every note and even the lyrics have been written.*

---

[10] Isaiah 41:10, Joshua 1:9, Psalm 32:8, Deuteronomy 31:8

Be on Your Way

But like any song, it's your choice to sing it.
This is not a solo performance.
This is a choir of music that needs every voice.
Don't be afraid to sing a wrong note. You can't. I use auto-tune.

    You're feeling pressed on every side, hoping not to be crushed.
    Yet a fragrant aroma arises when there's praise in the pressing.
It reaches my ears in a symphony as it restores your insight and understanding.

Align yourself to the rhythm of life infused by the running water of My Word —
not just babbling, but flooding —
created to bring ease of suffering, comfort of kindness,
exuberance of joyful sharing, and understanding the heart of God. Wow!

    You've been peddling (your faith), pedaling (uphill), paddling (upstream).
    Self-effort does not become you. Coast. Rest. Trust Me to remove,
    repair, and fine-tune, opening your heart to new rhythms.

Closed are the doors that lead to memories of pain and heartache.
The suffering did its work; no need to ruminate. Freedom of thought
and mobility surrounds your soul with new ideas and feelings. Plug into me.
    Get your fuel just from me for now.

Dear One, you're My Beloved.
I live inside you. You cannot run away from Me
    or hide anything from Me. Your sins are already forgiven.
    Asking Me to forgive you is your way of realizing that it's a done deal.
    Don't worry about tomorrow. It will take care of itself.

CHAPTER 7: How Far Can We Get on Fumes?

Just stay in My view, My Presence, and let Me comfort you.
Breathe. Be refreshed. Know that nothing can harm you
when I am your Protector, Defender, and Dad.
You are My chosen one. Get ready to walk straight,
shoulders back, tall, no shame, and pain-free.

It's time to redefine your job description. Here, let Me help you.
Your job description according to My Syllabus: Be at peace.
Trust Me. Worship Me. Enjoy Me.

Was that for you too? Was that really from God for His Church? If you feel like your gas gauge just got tapped into the reality zone of running on fumes, that's a good indication that it might have been. I think maybe this chapter has been a reminder for all of us to just take a minute and let God fill us back up, clean the windshield, and top off the oil.

You never know how long it's going to be to the next gas station.

CHAPTER 8: Is There Any Other Way?

There was a shortcut on a private "road" (if you can even call it that) back near the town line where I grew up. It really did save you about eight minutes of travel time if you could endure the peaks, gullies, and mystery puddles of ocean-depth proportions that needed navigating in order to get back onto the pavement again. I suspect the minefield of peril may actually have been strategically created by the few residents who lived along that 500-yard stretch. Their motivation was probably to deter drivers from cutting through their neighborhood, but I couldn't help but think they might have actually used it for entertainment, watching with binoculars as the unwanted cars disappeared into the potholes and small ponds they had masterfully created. For my dad, the "pass at your own risk" sign was simply an open invitation (more like a gauntlet challenge) for him to see how fast we could actually pass through the chamber of car-suspension

CHAPTER 8: Is There Any Other Way?

destruction without hitting our heads on the car ceiling or jarring any fillings out of our teeth. It was pretty fun!

My dad loved topographical maps. He did a lot of hiking and biking, and he knew how to study the terrain. He became quite adept at it. But each spring presented a new challenge. The winter snows and muddy March thaws (unless it really was just the neighbors mixing it up a bit) completely reformed that obstacle course, and the acclimation process had to begin all over again.

What's fun for some can be positively rattling to others, so using that shortcut was limited to rides when my mother was not in the car. She had lived through very rocky times already, so she preferred the longer, smoother route. For many of us we can relate to that longing for clear sailing. When hard winters and heavy rains make us feel like we're starting all over again, it can make us want to just stay put and avoid any more jolts at all cost. Even if it means missing out on getting to our destination more quickly, we feel compelled to protect ourselves from the inevitable jarring.

I'm trying to remember that time as a kid, before life, betrayal, disappointment, and pain, shook my sense of adventurous "risk-taking for-the-fun-of-it" out of me — back to when crazy bumps in the road made me giggle, and spinning till I was dizzy released endorphins, not adrenaline. It's part of the reconfiguring God is doing in me so I'll be ready for this next assignment. God has been working out of us anything holding us back, anything we may have misunderstood or picked up by mistake. He's covertly swapping them out for helpful ideas and habits — reprogramming, realigning, restoring, often without us even noticing. Even last week when you reached out to that person that was hard to reach out to, but you did it anyhow, that was training. Think back to that overwhelming project you started with absolutely no idea of how to get it done, but you stuck with it. You may have had to search out some help or advice (which in itself was humbling), but you did what it took to get it done. That was training. Have you noticed how recently you keep hearing whispers and nudges from God's Holy Spirit? They may even feel like your own thoughts at times, but surprisingly they're telling you to do something out of the ordinary for you, maybe at an unusual time for you to do it. You feel compelled enough to actually carry through with it. Again, it's training. God has been subtly preparing each of us to hear His voice and follow through without hesitation. It will need to be our default setting for this next assignment.

But some of our training gets so "intensive" it can feel more like punishment. We long for a way out, a time out, or a shortcut, no matter how bouncy. But the long, arduous way around was the very way we needed to go to be totally ready for our destination, and our destination was ready for us because we didn't get there too soon.

There are two Bible stories I'm thinking of that deal with taking shortcuts versus the long way around. One is Moses and the Israelites having to go the long way (40 years of the long way) to thin out the doubters and unbelievers in order to enter the promised land with great victory. And the other story is when Jesus took the shortcut through

CHAPTER 8: Is There Any Other Way?

Samaria that most Jews avoided by taking the usual long way around (due to bigotry) just so He could minister to one very broken Samaritan woman. His willingness to walk the path less traveled exposed an entire village to God's love. In both cases, the ways taken — long or short — each proved to be the hardest thing to do for the traveler, but in the end, the best thing to do.

When visiting my grandparents, my grandfather used to take my sister and me on great backyard adventures and across the street to the neighborhood park where we felt like we were exploring the other side of the world. Through wooded lots via overgrown paths, we navigated jungles of mountain-like mole hills, and thought we were conquering Everest. My grandfather was an itinerant preacher and loved to use every opportunity to teach and share from his heart. Whenever we would come to a fork in the path, one way heading straight up requiring navigation and stamina and the other way clearly marked and rock-free, he would say to us, scrunching up his nose and shaking his head side to side, "Do we want to go the easy way? Or..." with an excited gasp, wide eyes, and a big smile, "Or, do we want to go the hard way?" Obviously, "The hard way, Grampa, the hard way!" we'd squeal. To this day, as my sister and I talk about the trials and tribulations of life — sometimes caused by our own decisions — we conclude it's all Grampa Fred's fault. What was so bad about the easy way, again?

Years later when looking through my dad's things, I found a series of booklets his dad (my grandfather, Fred H. Bopp) had self-published in 1950 entitled, *Today's Challenge*. I had always known about them but never read them for myself. In the first booklet, subtitled *The Common-Sense Approach to Christianity*, I came to the last page of Chapter 3: *Facts Concerning Jesus*, and I was bowled over. Hand to my mouth, I gasped, "No way! There it is!" As I was reading this man's insightful thoughts, beautifully expressed, almost forgetting it was my Grampa Fred, I found myself starting to understand this man's heart. His heart was in the same church-reforming place 70 years ago that I find mine in today. As tempted as I am to just reprint his entire work, let me share just enough for now to explain my "no way" discovery moment.

The first couple pages of Chapter 3 describe, from a secular point of view, what we know about the man, Jesus, and who He appeared to be to the people of His day. He didn't really amount up to much from the world's perspective: He wasn't wealthy, well-educated, or endorsed by anyone in leadership. I loved how my grandfather then flips over our classic and iconic images of Jesus to expose what's underneath them. He writes:

> Such are the facts concerning Jesus Christ, and yet people ask why He does not have a place in secular history; why historians of His times either do not mention Him at all, or else dismiss Him with a sentence or two ... Certainly in this world of pain, intense physical suffering — even the agonizing suffering of crucifixion — does not entitle one to a place in history. Many other persons, before and after Jesus, experienced the tortures of this slow death ... There are unnamed, unnumbered thousands who have died in

CHAPTER 8: Is There Any Other Way?

the most intense pain after days, months, and even years of great suffering. There is nothing exceptional about the physical sufferings of Jesus that should set His name on the pages of secular history. He was not a hero martyr laying down his life as a patriot to free His people from the Roman yoke. Nor was He a religious zealot dying for the cause of His religion; not even for any system of teaching or principles was He being put to death. A personal issue had arisen between Himself and the religious leaders which aroused their jealousy and wrath, and because of this He was condemned to die ... Some ask whether Jesus should not have been given recognition by contemporary historians because He was the greatest teacher of all time ... [But] most of that which he taught was borrowed from the law and the prophets of the Old Testament, as He Himself stated, which He summed up in the Golden Rule. We are told that the Chinese had the Golden Rule (in negative form) hundreds of years before Jesus uttered it. His teaching, such as loving our enemies, turning the other cheek, going the second mile, which seems to carry us further than any previous teaching, was considered most impractical ... Still others ask whether Jesus should not have been given recognition because He is the world's superb example of right living. O the idealized Jesus! Has any character of history been more idealized than He? We have made Him to be the greatest and most wonderful in almost everything. He is our greatest preacher, our greatest teacher, our greatest humanitarian, and our greatest reformer. He is our greatest democrat, the greatest socialist, the greatest laborite, and also the greatest communist ... And so He is idealized as our perfect example by a church at ease while the world perishes; a church waxed fat and wealthy, surfeited with rank and titles, and quarreling with herself. It is so much easier to idealize Jesus than to follow Him; so much pleasanter to wear a cross than to bear one.

To the contemporary historian, He was not the idealized Jesus of the church today ... The only church the contemporary historian knew was the motley groups who were foolish enough to believe the claims of Jesus, and to follow Him in their way of life. They were simple enough to believe that Jesus was a preacher and teacher who practiced what He preached and taught. For them to make Jesus an example meant to obey His commandments. They were gullible enough so that instead of idealizing the Sermon on the Mount, they practiced it. *They took the hard way* and followed in the steps of Jesus. A few more centuries were to pass before the church would become sophisticated enough to *learn the easy way* — to idealize Jesus instead of following Him. The early church had not yet learned to "worship" Jesus instead of obeying Him.

And there it was! The hard way, Grampa, the hard way! I was in basic training before I even knew I had enlisted. To find out that this need to wake up, and to wake up my church family, is actually in my DNA — it inspired me.

CHAPTER 8: Is There Any Other Way?

As I read his booklet, inspired by his radical thinking, I wished I could sit down and talk to him now, to pick his brain and glean from all his life's experiences and ideas. Then it struck me, that's exactly what I was doing — reading pages of ideas he had felt so strongly about that he took the time to write them down. It was like having him right here with me. He even taught me new vocabulary words like "practicable" and "surfeit." I'm going to try to slip those into conversations more. What can I say? He always loved to teach.

Grampa was the one who paid us to memorize Bible verses when we were kids. Those are the verses I remember best, and I know which verses they are because I memorized them in the King James Version. That's all we had back in the 60s. Like Mary Poppins, he made games out of chores: Okay now, who can pick up the most horse chestnuts and how far can you throw them into the woods before Grammy calls us in for dinner? Sometimes the winner got to take home a treasure consisting of trinkets and odds-and-ends that Grampa had no use for but, according to him, still had life in them. We thought we hit the jackpot. My mom just rolled her eyes, bit her tongue, and looked for opportunity to find just the right place to bury all that "treasure."

In my teens and twenties, I remember having talks with my grandfather. I didn't realize the value of the gems he was sharing with me. After I married, he came to lead a few neighborhood Bible studies at our new home. People were fascinated with his stories and his wisdom. I didn't see it so much then. I thought, "That's just Grampa

Be on Your Way

Fred, being Grampa Fred. He's old. He knows stuff." I just didn't understand the treasure that he was.

After reading the introduction to *Today's Challenge,* that "These three booklets have already been published. Series 4 will be ready for publication (D.V.) by summer of 1950..." I wondered if God has passed the baton on to me in what feels like the last leg of the race. You see, I don't believe My grandfather's fourth booklet ever made it to print. He describes it: "In it is emphasized *The Adequacy of Christian Faith*, and a practicable outline is presented of what we as individuals and groups can do to further the cause of Christian faith through victorious Christian living." Could *Be on Your Way* turn out to be that outline of what we as individuals and groups can do to further the cause of Christian faith? That would be so awesome! I pray for that outcome. The same introduction printed in each of his booklets, ends with this paragraph:

> In a time midst cold wars and uncertainty when peace and security are longingly desired, we trust that we shall accept *Today's Challenge*, and that in Jesus Christ "of whom, through whom, and unto whom are all things" we shall become more than conquerors.

A prophetic friend of ours just told my husband Steve, as they were praying together, that he had a vision of Steve in an old silver warplane with the door open. Steve was standing in the opening and the pilot was telling him to jump. He was like a Navy SEAL in this vision, one who would be the first sent covertly into enemy territory. SEALs are

CHAPTER 8: Is There Any Other Way?

intensively trained, but still he was afraid to jump. Even so, because the pilot told him to jump, he did. When Steve described the vision to me, I instantly envisioned myself in the doorway and felt that flip-flop in my stomach when you're about to do something you're afraid to do. I've actually been feeling that way in real life for some time now. I was kind of glad that I wasn't in the vision because if I had been, I don't think I could have jumped. Then I pictured some tandem-skydivers, with the experienced instructor strapped behind the student to make sure all goes well. And I thought, now *that* I think I could do. We have been trained by an Expert who is not only telling us to jump, but is strapped to us ready to jump with us, guiding our every move. We may be jumping into the unknown to do something we're not sure we are ready to do, but God knows that we are and it's time.

Getting to this point may have taken a very wearisome long time. It may have been an incredibly bumpy shortcut with a surfeit of deep ravines that almost swallowed us. There may have been practicable, easier paths to follow, smooth, well-marked, but they were not an option for us.

Because Someone we love and trust asked us if we wanted to go the hard way ... and we said yes.

CHAPTER 9: Do You Have a Reservation?

When trying to hear what God wanted me to write next, and for days not knowing where to go from here, I finally asked Him maybe could He give me the *title* of Chapter 9 (since that's how this whole book got started, by hearing just the title). Can't hurt to ask. And within minutes, *Do You Have a Reservation?* is what went down on the paper. And yay, it kept in line with the travel theme — Hotel or restaurant reservations, and RSVP's. Then my thoughts turned to special events, saving a spot, a time, a place. But then I realized it could also refer to having second thoughts or feeling doubtful, having reservations. Next, I chuckled because it also sounded like I was asking a Native American where they might be living. I'm sorry if that's not politically correct, but I needed to include it because of what it all confirmed for me, as you will see.

CHAPTER 9: Do You Have a Reservation?

When I looked up the definition for reservation, I discovered that my interpretations of the title/question came in the exact order that the top three usages of the word were listed: 1. Saving a place or time 2. Having doubt or hesitation, and 3. Land set aside for Native Americans. I realized that "Do you have a reservation?" was a loaded question and it was more than a title. It was being directed to *me*.

So, it's time to confess: Days ago, as I started thinking about what to write next, I thought God was telling me to tell you about an idea that I had some time back. But I had "reservations" about sharing it with you. It feels too much like it's in its infancy stages right now, almost experimental, no proven method or conclusive outcome, and me being raised in the science age, I didn't think it was worthy to publish. I guess God thinks otherwise.

I stated in the Introduction of this book it wasn't going to be about some cleverly designed method of "Doing Church." I still want that to be true. But I also asked God to reveal to us practical ways to get where we're going. Why don't we look at this next idea not as a suggestion but more as me just sharing with you what "being on *my* way" is looking like so far for me.

Summer 2019 is when God spoke to me about writing *Be on Your Way*. And so it began. Chapter by chapter and into November, after writing how important it is to God for us all to be using our gifts, being led by the Spirit in unison, and how we needed to break out of the old spectator/consumer mentality, I asked God what it would take. How could we possibly, practically speaking, help people break free from these natural tendencies and habits we've developed in group-settings? When it's obvious God is calling all of us into something much greater and very different, but most of us feel perfectly content following a matter of course, safe and familiar, how do we even begin to coax ourselves and others into new possibilities? Even if we're determined to be different, and plan on being spontaneous, we tend to gravitate back to the familiar. We're such creatures of habit. Just think about how awkward it feels, even in your own living room, to sit in the other chair because a guest sat in your spot. You feel like you're just about in a whole different house, right? You can't wait for them to leave, or at least excuse themselves for a minute, so you can swoop in and settle back into your comfy seat in order to bring balance back to your universe.

A familiar and common expectation of really any gathering in our culture is that the host, or whoever organized the get-together, runs the show. They are the ones the guests look to for their cue as to what to do next. For example, Bible studies and church home-groups are typically orchestrated by a designated leader to whom everyone looks to keep the conversation lively, to ask the important questions. Or, sometimes when a "non-leader" with lots to say dominates a discussion, the rest of the group looks desperately to the leader to stop the manipulation. Any person in that group is more than capable of chiming in, but somehow that would be going against some unwritten protocol. How can we help a room full of people, who are well trained to attend a meeting and speak only when called on, or only when they think they have the "right" answer (meaning the specific answer that

CHAPTER 9: Do You Have a Reservation?

the leader/teacher is looking for) to break free from that mindset? What will help them understand that they each have gifts and ideas to share with the group that are unique and just as important as everyone else's? Each member is an important component of God's iridescent spectrum. If someone doesn't show up, that beacon of promise is incomplete.

If we each carry God's Holy Spirit within us, and are gifted according to His wisdom and impartation of those gifts, then we should be able to minister to one another so beautifully there would be no need to have any other leader besides Him. The Holy Spirit is the most perfect of all Leaders. He has supernatural ways to direct, choreograph, and teach each of us, using all who are willing to be used. But, being led by the Spirit as a group? What would that look like, and how in the world would we get us from here to there? Can we really think that far outside the box? And then I heard, "It's almost Christmas. Just *open* the box. The gifts are inside. Church is meant to be a gift exchange."

A gift exchange, yeah … I like that. Then, all I could picture was a "Yankee Gift Swap." If you're not familiar with the term, it's a kind of gift exchange where everybody brings an untagged, but wrapped mystery present. Some gifts are really nice and some are outrageously silly, whatever the guest chooses to bring. Everyone takes a number to get started and then, in order of the numbers drawn, each person takes a turn opening any gift they want. As their turn comes, if they'd rather "steal" an already opened gift they like from the person who opened it, participants have the option to "swap their turn." They can take the opened gift and let the guest whose gift they "stole" have a chance to open another present instead.

Now I know the casting of lots in Scripture stopped being written about when the Holy Spirit was poured into Jesus's followers at Pentecost, but numbers being drawn at a gift swap still sounds fun to me. And, it may be familiar enough to the people coming (who might be stuck in a pattern) that it wouldn't feel too new and scary as it helped pull us out of a rut. What if everyone who comes to a church gathering brings their spiritual gifts to swap — a song of worship, a Scripture, a testimony, a word of knowledge, healing and miracles, something they read that touched their heart — whatever they have to give away that will encourage, edify, and build up the others who have come? Everyone could pick out a number at the start of our time together, a number that would give us an order of when it's our turn to offer our "present" to the group. It could work. It could get us into a different way of experiencing what Scriptures called "the gathering together."

We read in Acts 2:42-47 that:

They devoted themselves to the apostles teaching and to the fellowship, to the breaking of bread and to prayer. Everyone was filled with awe, and many wonders and miraculous signs were done by the apostles. All the believers were together and had everything in common. Selling their possessions and goods, they gave to anyone as he had need. Every day they continued to meet together

CHAPTER 9: Do You Have a Reservation?

in the temple courts. They broke bread in their homes and ate together with glad and sincere hearts, praising God and enjoying the favor of all the people. And the Lord added to their number daily those who were being saved.

The early church pooled their resources to make sure no one had any unmet needs. What if a bag for offerings and contributions would be left on the counter? People could slip their money in whenever. Then whoever pulled the number marked with a star would be in charge that day of any collected money. That person could take and keep the money if they needed it, give it away and bless whomever God directed them to bless, invest it, or leave it there to build up for the next meeting.

I've heard it argued that even though breaking bread is given as one of the very reasons the church gathered together (in verse 42) and refers to taking Communion, some feel that the daily breaking of bread together in homes (mentioned in verse 46) refers simply to eating a meal together. Even if that were the case, what matters most is that they got together daily and lived life together, in communion. They didn't have phones to check in on each other, so they gathered often. They broke bread and had communion. Whether it refers to daily receiving Holy Communion or simply enjoying the communion of each other's company by living life together, it points us in the right direction of navigating effectively as a church family.

What do most families gather around? Okay, no, not the TV. Where do most families gather to eat, and which meal is it that they typically share? As a church family, wouldn't it make sense to gather at the Lord's Supper Table? Whenever it is you choose to remember and proclaim the Lord's death until He comes, I strongly feel that recognizing the power of the Body and Blood of Jesus while taking Communion together is vitally important to staying healthy both spiritually and physically and should be taken advantage of as often as you can. It is a gift from Jesus with supernatural benefits and is mandated by Him for our sakes. We should make sure that at some point during every gathering we recognize the Body and Blood of Jesus and receive the restorative benefits of remembering Him by taking in the bread and the cup, together as a family.

If we take our cue from the early church, we see that they still maintained their Jewish tradition of praying three times a day in the temple courts. They honored the laws and traditions of the old covenant; they knew them by heart. But now they devoted themselves to learning and living by the *new* covenant of grace, the teaching and instructions of Jesus, who took the law to a whole new level of living, making it all about heart attitude, mercy, and forgiveness. They would read letters from missionaries and apostles that encouraged and instructed them. They would use discernment and practice accountability when hearing each other's ideas, teachings, and experiences, in order to filter out confusion or falsehood.

Did some of the churches fall prey to false teaching? Yes. Did their gathering together protect them from making mistakes? Did breaking bread daily make them perfect examples of Christian living?

CHAPTER 9: Do You Have a Reservation?

Obviously not. But do you know what it did do? It added souls to the Kingdom of God by the thousands. It made them strong and courageous enough to die in the Coliseum, or on stakes and crosses standing firm for their beliefs and devotion to Jesus without wavering. It made them glad to give up land, homes, and life for the Truth of the resurrected Messiah, rejoicing that they were counted worthy to share in the sufferings of Christ. It spread the news like fire that the Kingdom of Heaven is accessible to Jew and Gentile, and that King Jesus is a Savior who shares with us His authority and power to overcome all fear and darkness. It gave them the determination to heal the sick, raise the dead, cleanse the leper, and preach the good news as far as they could travel, baptizing nations in the Name of Jesus. It let them live life to the full — affirmed, belonging, and loved. I want that. I called a few friends to run the gift swap idea past them. They didn't think it was as off the wall as I thought they would.

I'm forever grateful for those people God has placed in my life who have stuck by me and supported me through so many seasons. After tearing ourselves away from our friends and Faith family in 2012 in order to pursue God's purpose for us, we were blessed to find an authentic, Spirit-filled group of believers who loved us and helped us heal. They encouraged us on our journey and lovingly sent us on our way when it was time to move on. This in no way reflects negatively on any of our past church friends, but for the years since serving with them, I've been longing to find my new tribe.

Be on Your Way

I wanted to be known again and accepted just as I am, and to know and accept others without reservation or criticism. I've been looking for comrades to whom I didn't have to explain myself or how I believed. I yearned to be able to gather with people who didn't think exactly like me, but who didn't care that we didn't think exactly alike about everything, as long as we followed Jesus and were led by His Holy Spirit, operating in His gifts and power. I had prayed to find a fellowship of people that I could go to war with and know they would have my back, as I had theirs.

And that's why belonging to a reservation, a land set aside for my tribe in which we could freely live and breathe, was an important part of the definition for me. As we visited church gatherings here and there, we met dear brothers and sisters in Christ, but no place felt like home. I started to get the sense that my new tribe was not going to be led by a chief. It was destined to be led by a King.

In December, we started meeting in a friend's new home. She had been instructed by God the year before — actually given a vision — that if she bought the house God would fill it. We have been drawing numbers, worshiping by sharing our gifts and ideas, pooling our resources, taking Communion together, praying, laughing, enjoying each other's company, and wondering what God is going to do next. We've been amused and amazed by how the Holy Spirit has coordinated our gifts, offerings and efforts. We're encouraged by how beautifully the flow of each meeting goes, and how refreshed we feel as we leave. It's only been a couple months since we started meeting

CHAPTER 9: Do You Have a Reservation?

on the first and third Sunday afternoons. My hope is, as we settle in, that we will not fall into a pattern of having to rely on the numbers to direct the order of things, but that we will all be so in tune enough with our Father's heart, and with each other, that we'll be able to walk in step, in unison.

My hesitation to share this with you (besides being in the infancy stage) was that it could seem like this is the new way I think we should all do church. This is not a method or step by step plan. It's just our attempt to listen, take a risk, and give something new a try. God is doing something new, but He never asks us to do something He hasn't prepared us for. Sometimes it feels like you're standing in the open door of an airplane. Sometimes it feels like you're holding your breath with your eyes closed, inches away from a cake full of lit candles, daring to make a wish, daring to dream again after so many disappointments, daring to believe in the God who makes impossible dreams come true.

Do I have a reservation? As I've written this down for you, I've realized that God is in the process of answering my heart's cry for a tribe. A special place has been set aside for me to be with them. I will be missed if I don't show up, as will they. I feel as if my spot has been saved for me, a time has been reserved.

It would appear that, yes, I have a reservation. Do you?

CHAPTER 10: Are You Hungry Yet?

I'm reaching down deep inside of me to a feeling that has no words yet. There are some emotions best expressed poetically; others call for lots of bold capital letters and strong determined words. Writing them down, streaming them without a filter, just transferring feelings onto paper, can be so cathartic. I wish I had the words to paint the colors I'm sensing today, but it seems the only color I can see at the moment is gray — steely, like armor-and-swords gray. I think God is keeping the darkness at bay and I'm experiencing His protection, but I'm hearing, sensing, and feeling the clashing of kingdoms only feet away from me. From all different directions I keep being told, "God's fighting on your behalf."

Everywhere I glance, especially when talking and praying with people, I can see God doing amazing work in them. I assure them He is hearing every prayer and catching every tear. He is in control and

CHAPTER 10: Are You Hungry Yet?

still on His Throne no matter what circumstances are shouting at us. I know with all my heart that He is working all things together for our benefit. Yet at the same time, I can completely relate to their fear, confusion and uncertainty. As I ask God for clarity and wisdom to enlighten and encourage so many who feel blind-sided in this season, I realize that the comfort and advice that flow out of my mouth are not just for my friends. Even if the words offered are not well received by them, it's okay, because I see now, they were really intended for me.

I'm realizing that there are some words and ideas God offers us that are meant to be eaten slowly, chewed on, and digested, but you have to be pretty hungry, more like practically starving, in order to swallow some of them. God keeps reminding me of the line in the confirmation poem: Come to the stove with empty plate. It's empty alright. And there's a rumbling that needs to be satisfied.

One of my desires in writing this, has been to offer words that would somehow move you and me into unison, and into a place that our Father wants us to be: the place where we "play nice," work hard, and enjoy supper together as a family. But are we hungry enough yet? "Come to the stove with empty plate" sounded so silly to me when I scribbled it down that morning all those months ago. God knew I would need it in this moment. I'm starting to see that the "grayness" of battle that I'm sensing is actually a catalyst that's causing hunger pangs, not only in me, but on a much, much bigger scale.

As I have arrived at this chapter, the world is in the process of responding to a global outbreak of COVID-19 (the Coronavirus).

Be on Your Way

If you live anywhere on this planet, I don't have to explain that it's a very contagious virus that can affect a person's respiratory system. Years from now, this moment may go the way of the swine-flu and Y2K scenarios and hardly be thought of again. But in my lifetime, I have not seen this much panic over anything else. I was not alive during the world wars, and I'm not sure if social media has exacerbated the public's response, but this panic feels epic somehow.

The virus itself appears no worse than the flu in most cases, except that it is new and no one has built up immunity to it yet. But it's being presented to us as a sinister plague, out of control, lurking around every corner. Borders are closing around the world. Two weeks of quarantine are being imposed on anyone coming home from another country. Our nation is all working from home. It's springtime here but schools are closed until further notice, and colleges are being taught online. It's been ordered that people shelter at home, which has led to most churches having to only stream their Sunday services online instead of meeting in person. Regular churchgoers find themselves gathering with their households to watch and worship together from their homes. Hmm… imagine that.

Being told to shelter at home and not gather, not even with family that doesn't reside with you, feels pretty drastic. But does absence really make the heart grow fonder? Are we hungry yet?

A special National Day of Prayer was declared by Donald J. Trump, President of the United States, as models projected a serious mortality rate from the virus. The nation was encouraged to call

CHAPTER 10: Are You Hungry Yet?

on God against this invisible enemy. And Christians were called by prophetic church leaders to a worldwide, three-day fast of repentance to pull down strongholds of fear and command the virus to go. This virus, and its accompanying fear, must die as God's Church wakes up and courageously declares victory over it.

I can't help but think that this crisis we're dealing with, flung at us by the enemy (obviously trying to stop God's coming prophesied revival, and evangelistic stadium gatherings from happening) is being turned around by our loving Lord, the Commander of Angel Armies, to prepare the troops and unite His people. And here I was trying to figure out how in the world God was going to unite His global Church.

I had heard a prophetic word spoken months ago that Baby Boomers (born 1946-1964) were going to play a pivotal role in this new move of God. Our maturity, wisdom, and moral standards are necessary to pray and impact this generation — this nation — with God's good intentions for them. This particular virus, like the flu, causes the most severe cases among seniors, as well as those with underlying conditions or compromised immune systems. It's interesting to me. Our president's administration has set up guidelines and restrictions to preserve and protect us Baby Boomers, out of respect and consideration. Some people feel the restrictions are limiting and unfair. But the guidelines feel to me more like God's favor and preservation in the middle of an unfair global attack.

Above and beyond the cloud of media reports and "words on the street" is God's promise of provision, power, and peace amid this time of preparation. Alliteration aside, the purpose emphasized to me was preparation. As much of the world is feeling this is a plague of punishment, I actually believe it is an enemy attack that God is turning around to better prepare us. He is forcing us to rest, reflect, and reform. He is about to hit reset.

The real epidemic is the rampant fear that is causing anxiety and hopelessness. Now, for people who don't know Jesus, I can totally understand it. But I'm talking about all the people I know who do know Jesus. Fear is our biggest roadblock to where God wants to take us. I knew I had to work this roadblock topic in somewhere because of something my husband had said that really impressed me. He was retelling part of the conversation he had regarding church leaders not wanting to overtax people's schedules, not wanting to inconvenience them or demand too much of their time. The person with whom he was talking said something like, we don't want to cause any roadblocks for people, to which Steve replied, "Schedules are only roadblocks if you're not passionate." That was deep. I made him repeat it so I could write it down.

Right now, everyone's schedule has been interrupted. Everyone's passion has turned to not catching a virus while maintaining an income, as well as some inexplicable "passionate concerns" that have unexpectedly come to the surface during a panic-induced viral shopping frenzy.

What are you passionate about right now? What are you hungry for? I'll tell you what the people in these United States are the most

CHAPTER 10: Are You Hungry Yet?

passionate about — Toilet paper. Crazy, right? During this declared national emergency, the stores and online suppliers have been wiped out of toilet paper (pun unintended, but I thought I'd leave it in). Here in our neck of the woods, we are obviously passionate about frozen vegetables as well. That part of the store freezer was as empty as the paper goods aisle. Understandably, sanitizer, paper towels, and cleaning supplies have disappeared. But frozen veggies? Who'd have thought?

I think this global "crisis" is going to be used by God to deal with this blockage, make us hungry again, and reopen the road to beyond-our-imagination possibilities. Trusting Him through this global reset phase is the most important part of the process. Trust equals rest in my vocabulary. Resting in the shadow of the Almighty, abiding in His Presence, brings perfect peace. God will keep in perfect peace those whose minds are steadfast, because they trust in Him.[11] We're going to get past this roadblock if we stay passionate. And because of Jesus, we will be unscathed; trusting moment by moment, remembering that whatever we focus on becomes bigger while the rest diminishes. So in faith and passionate trust, we keep our eyes on Jesus. Stepping into His perfect love allows Him to cast out all fear, and faith trumps fear.

In the middle of this mandated nationwide work-from-home and practice-social-distancing phase of the "panic-demic," I texted a friend to see how she was doing. Her reply brought such balance back to me. She texted, "I kind of like being stuck at home. I'm feeling quite

---

[11] See Isaiah 26:3

peaceful. I may need to work, but I feel restful." Restful. I told her that was beautiful and I was going to adopt that feeling. Have you ever had just one word flood chapters of meaning into your spirit? She had just spoken balance back into my teeter-tottering world with that one word — restful.

Resting in the fact that God is in charge and that the power of His Spirit is at work within us, gives us an anchor to hold onto when waves of statistics and fear of the unknown toss us around. Those waves can feel very big. Those waves *are* very big at this moment. This is when our faith meets fear and must wrestle it to the ground by reminding it of God's faithfulness and perfect love.

Even though the roadblock sign and barrier look huge, it's as if God just posted a detour sign to take us to our destination via another way — a better way that will really prepare us, and refresh our skills, and hone our ability to recognize His signs. Somewhere in these unexpected twists and turns we are supposed to be learning to keep our eyes more open, to look in the rearview mirror at ourselves and ask, "Do you really believe in everything you claim to believe?"

Psalm 91 says we will tread upon the lion and cobra. We will trample the great lion and the serpent. "Because he loves me," says the Lord, "I will rescue him. I will protect him for he acknowledges my name..." And I know that Scripture by heart. We're being asked to believe without actually seeing the outcome, that everything is going to be better than okay, because God is still directing our path, still watching over us, still true to His Word. But this is really hard.

CHAPTER 10: Are You Hungry Yet?

I guess it would be less challenging to see if I stopped covering my eyes and put my hands back on the steering wheel, huh? I thought I was doing well for myself because it was hard enough not being sure of where we were actually headed — uncertainty can be so uncomfortable — and still I was willing to go. But wherever it was, wherever it still is, the backroads are feeling a bit overwhelming at the moment. There are too many corners that things could be hiding behind, and it's been a while since I've seen the orange detour arrows. Did I miss something?

He's using this global testing like a pop quiz so we'll be better abled and prepared for the final exam — the one that really counts. And I'm not talking prepared for the next bigger pandemic; I'm talking about trusting Him and following every sign, every direction He shows us, so we will be trained and ready for the greatest revival ever experienced on this planet. That is what is truly hiding behind the next corner. God has been showing me my test results, using this time to reveal to me where I'm not really trusting Him, not to shame me, but to instruct me as to where my weak spots are and what He'll be working on in me, with my permission. This could take a while. In the meantime, His words of courage[12] sustain me:

1. *Be still*, and know that I am God.
2. *Fear not*, for I am with you.
3. *Take heart*, for I have overcome the world.

---

[12] For the complete verses see Psalm 46:10, Isaiah 41:10, John 16:33

Be on Your Way

It may sound bizarre, but God is telling me that in the middle of a global pandemic we should not only be at peace, we should be excited. It's not about being in denial. It's not living in some alternate reality... or maybe it is.

I looked up alternate reality to find it refers to a parallel universe — a realm of existence and experience that is fundamentally different from the one that most humans share, a separate reality. I'm treading in territory beyond my expertise here, but I think that describes what I'm feeling like today. Knowing that we live in two realms at the same time (physical and spiritual) makes me think that "alternate reality" isn't such a bad description. It could appear to some that I'm an ostrich. But like some favorite stories of mine portray (one about Santa, and one about building a baseball field instead of planting a corn crop), what God is showing me is that seeing isn't believing, believing is seeing.

Hebrew 11:1 says that "faith is being sure of what we hope for and certain of what we do not see." But what about being certain of what we do see that nobody else around us seems to see? I love that in the 2 Kings (chapter 6) account of the prophet Elisha and his servant being surrounded by the enemy, Elisha also saw God's greater heavenly army surrounding the enemy. His servant saw nothing but certain doom, until Elisha asked God to show him the alternate reality and the servant's spiritual eyes were open to see a vast angelic army about to fight on their behalf. What I admire most is that the servant's fear and doubt didn't seem to faze Elisha's certainty of what he saw. I'm

CHAPTER 10: Are You Hungry Yet?

praying for that kind of unwavering certainty in the hope and peace God is placing in me.

Whatever God is doing to unite His people, His Bride, I'm born and bred for this moment. So are you. We're part of this whole story of His. We have been closed in, like Moses, by the Hand of God covering us in the cleft of a rock as He passes by. God is about to show us His glory. We're about to celebrate Passover closed in with just the members of our household. For some that means by themselves. But for each of us who know Messiah Jesus, we will celebrate freedom and eat our meals behind our doors that are covered by the Blood of the Lamb, just like Moses and the Hebrew slaves about to be delivered. We are about to see the glory and mighty Hand of God for ourselves.

But God doesn't just want to show us this time. He wants to fill us so we are able to carry and demonstrate His glory in order to transform all the nations of this world. We were born for this. It's about making disciples of all nations. Have you been feeling it too? The awareness of a bigger picture, a national one, is becoming more in focus now. Our call is to pray for the healing of our nation so we can promote the healing of other nations. That's what this global shaking is all about. God's getting rid of everything that is taking up much needed space, increasing our personal capacity to hold more of Him, and shoring up our very foundations. We're His National Guards and we're being called into active duty.

Be on Your Way

We need to be able to stand under the awesomeness of His incredible glory and bring it to the leaders of our communities, our government officials, and people of influence. We may not be famous or well-known ourselves, but we're bound to know somebody who knows somebody else, whose barber is related to the mayor's cousin, and the ripple effect can be a very powerful one especially when boosted along by our connections in very High Places. God will make sure it reaches the top. We also have a Commander Who never assigns us a mission without making a way to complete it. We just have to choose to accept it!

This is an unprecedented time. I keep hearing "unprecedented" from all angles: The shutdown of our nation and at least 184 other nations to a virus — unprecedented. Weather patterns, world records, the suicide rate, opioid crisis, lack of morality — all unprecedented. But to trump it all is the prophesied unprecedented move of Father God's love for the nations.

Churches have taken to the airwaves. Social media and the internet, a global community once ruled by the prince of this world, have suddenly been filled with prayer meetings, church services, and Bible studies. What was once a platform for harmful lies and visual addictions has been overrun with worship, testimonies, and prayer. It appears that God has prepared a table before us in the presence of our enemies.

Tell me, are you hungry yet?

CHAPTER 11: Is it Time to Stretch?

I have vacationed in the White Mountains of New Hampshire every summer or fall since I was a kid: camping, hiking, biking, horseback riding, exploring, taking old-fashioned scenic train rides. And of course, there was looking for moose — so many "moose crossing" and giant "watch for moose" signs posted, all practically guaranteeing a moose sighting, you'd think you wouldn't have to look so hard to spot one, but you do.

My heart does a little dance just thinking about the mountains. As fun as it's always been, and as sweet as it is adventuring with my children sharing favorite places together and now introducing their children to them as well; beyond all the adventure and fun of it lies this immense connection I feel with those awesome White Mountains. It can only be described as spiritual. When they finally come into view,

CHAPTER 11: Is it Time to Stretch?

after the long drive, I take a deep breath and sigh; the travel-weariness just melts away because I feel like … Ah… now this is home.

Depending on the time of day we travel, the traffic can make the trip feel especially long. We have a rest stop at which we traditionally take a break, located about an hour away from our destination. But one year, we had left home just after breakfast and were making such good time, neither of us felt the need to stop. We decided to keep driving right on through to our favorite pizza place in Lincoln for lunch. We were excited to get there sooner rather than later because we had only eaten a light breakfast and our goodie bag of sweet and salty snacks just wasn't as appealing for morning travel.

There's a stretch of highway just south of the mountains that's posted: dangerous crosswinds. I love that sign because it means we are almost there. We're just minutes from seeing the quaint New Hampshire village in the valley below and the "Welcome Home" mountainous greeting of the silhouetted peaks just beyond the next bend.

Without taking that usual rest-stop break, we were at that sign in record time. We braved through the perfectly calm "dangerous crosswinds," and like Pavlov's dog both started salivating for our favorite pizza. We could almost smell it. Mountains waved "hello" to me, but what waved more nobly (and almost frantically) at me that year, was the flapping flag marked O-P-E-N, beckoning us to lunch. We skidded like a stock car racer into the parking lot, opened our car doors simultaneously, and hopped out. At least we tried to hop out;

my legs were numb and felt as if they might be permanently bent in the seated position, even though I was telling them to straighten out. In fact, I actually looked down at them to see if they were still there. I glanced over at Steve who was standing next to the car but still holding onto the door for support. We both started to laugh as we, with great determination, put one foot in front of the other like tinmen without an oil can to be had, driven forward by sheer strength of will, the promise of pizza and its tantalizing aroma moving us ever onward. We may have arrived in time for lunch, but it looked and felt like we may not actually make it into the building to place our order much before supper. "I guess skipping the rest stop wasn't the best idea, huh?" Traditions become traditions for a reason, I suppose.

We need to stretch every once in a while, especially before the last leg of the race. If you are wanting to get from the parking lot into the restaurant before they close (or before the young owners who hung the open flag that morning begin collecting a pension) get out of the car and take a stretch somewhere along the way.

Have you ever noticed how a good stretch in the morning, just before you get out of bed, can actually make you feel so content and relaxed that you feel like you could go back to sleep? You hold your breath, scrunch your shoulders, and move slightly side to side, then like a cat waking from a nap, you reach out with your hands and even your toes as if testing the water, then exhale with a satisfied sigh or yawn. Why does stretching make you feel so good? I looked up the answer — endorphins. And who doesn't like endorphins? Stretching

CHAPTER 11: Is it Time to Stretch?

actually releases them and also rushes a new oxygenated blood-supply to the muscles you are stretching. It's important before any prolonged physical activity to gently stretch your muscles so they are prepared to work out. It makes them more flexible and able to move more freely, and less prone to injury. God thought of everything — something so important that He attached a feel-good hormone to it.

But there is a kind of stretch that doesn't usually feel so good: the physical-therapy kind of stretching after an injury or surgery. It actually helps repair and rebuild the muscles but there's no endorphins to be felt. Coaching, determination, and pushing through the pain to reach the goal of recovery are what motivate that kind of stretching.

In both cases, stretching is important and necessary. I much prefer the morning stretch to the physical therapy kind, thank you very much. But here we are, the body of Christ. Some parts of us are just waking up. Others have been injured and require a bit of coaching and a lot of encouragement. Parts of us are doing that limb-shaking thing an athlete does before a big event when they will be demanding full cooperation from every disciplined muscle in their body. This is a time of shaking for sure. God is stretching each of us. He's teaching us how to be more flexible. Pushing through the pain is part of the recovery regimen. He's waking us up and breathing new life into this Body of His. But this is a really big event we're about to step into and take on. It will demand full cooperation from every disciplined muscle we have. Each of us, each person, each community, each nation, has a vital role in this leg of the race. They tell me so much of athletic achievements are accomplished by using the muscle located between your ears. Your brain, your mindset, really determines the outcome.

I'm not sure exactly when I started (probably around my 40th birthday), but a couple months before the actual anniversary of my birth I would try the year on for size, and in my thinking, or if someone asked my age, I would tell them the number of my upcoming year (probably so it wouldn't feel like such a shock when I actually got there). Remember as kids, if someone asked how old we were, we'd respond with eight and three quarters, or almost nine. We were so anxious to be as old as we could be. Jumping ahead to the next year's number, for me now, isn't because I want to be older than I am. It's more about just getting used to the new number so when asked my age, I won't have to constantly do the math from the year I was born to the present day. Years don't hold your attention like they used to. So maybe you do the same as I do, and think ahead in the hopes that when asked how many candles you want on your cake you will be able to answer appropriately. Okay, I have to confess that there was one year I started so far ahead of my birthday that on my actual birthday I felt for a minute that I had advanced ahead two years. It was a fleeting moment, but it showed me the power our thinking patterns can have on us.

God is asking us to stretch our thinking pattern in this new era for which He has been preparing us. Being on our way into unexplored territory takes a pioneer spirit and all kinds of stretching. Stretching your thinking can seem painful at first, but eventually it will cause your

CHAPTER 11: Is it Time to Stretch?

endorphins to dance again. We interrupt this reading moment with a brief pop-up infomercial from our sponsors:

"You can't afford to miss this Destination Package Deal!"

Great news! You have an opportunity of a lifetime to sign up for an all-expense paid one-way trip to some place absolutely amazing! We think. We haven't actually been there yet. But we've heard that it's pretty amazing. We can't tell you when your departure date will be, or exactly how you'll be traveling. In fact, you may be flying solo, or possibly with millions of others all at the same time. The good news is that it's paid for and it'll get you out of this mundane, ho-hum existence! You just have to follow a few simple instructions and abide by the rules for the entire rest of your life. So we can't tell you what your destination is for sure, but we can guarantee you that there's a 50/50 chance you're going to love it ... eventually ... if you sign up today that is, and don't back out last minute. So you better sign up now, don't you think? What are you waiting for? Plus ... to be honest, I could really use the commission. So ... come on, what do you say?

You may not recognize the sales pitch, but this is how I've often heard the "gospel message" presented. It's a very misguided way of thinking, and sadly very prevalent in a lot of Christian circles, and it pretty much promotes the idea that if you don't sign up by praying the sinner's prayer, your dream destination turns into a permanent vacation from hell. And yes, it's free; Jesus paid for your salvation, that's true. What that means to some is "you can know that eventually it'll get you to heaven when you die, if you don't mess up. And you can't just sit there. You've got to do, do, do, because as you know, faith without works is dead. Also there are rules and regulations, ways to prove your faith is genuine, ways to work out your salvation with fear and trembling." You can almost hear the presenter add: Show us "the fruit" so we'll know if we can take credit for you "getting saved" or not.

I'm not sure where or when that technique was crafted, but I'm pretty sure you can't find it anywhere in the Bible. In fact, when asked, "What must I do to be saved?" the Apostle Paul and his friend Silas responded, "Believe in the Lord Jesus and you will be saved — you and your household" (Acts 16:30). Paul also wrote in Romans 10:9-10 that: "If you declare with your mouth, 'Jesus is Lord,' and believe in your heart that God raised him from the dead, you will be saved. For it is with your heart that you believe and are justified, and it is with your mouth that you profess your faith and are saved." Sounds pretty simple, doesn't it? How did it become so complicated?

Partly to blame is the fact we've been taught alternate meanings of important words. We've been led to believe that "eternal life" is another term for "going to heaven after we die," when in actuality, the Greek word in the New Testament translated in many cases to "eternal" is more accurately translated "abundant." It's a quality of life not a quantity. The people of the Jewish culture who were alive to see Jesus' here in the flesh, were all expecting God's Kingdom to come here to this planet. Heaven was not thought to be our eternal living

CHAPTER 11: Is it Time to Stretch?

quarters up in the heavens somewhere. Old Testament prophecies teach it will be here on our own renewed earthly planet (See Isaiah 65:17-25 & 66:22-23). When they would ask Jesus about inheriting eternal life, they were asking about being included in the forever Kingdom of the prophesied Messiah who will reign over the entire world from Jerusalem. And "salvation" is a word that also has a much deeper meaning than just the forgiveness of our sins and keeping us out of hell. The Greek word for salvation is "sozo," and it's meaning carries the promise of physical healing and being delivered from demonic torment here and now, not when we die. The questions "What must I do to be saved?" and "How do I inherit eternal life?" aren't really about "getting to heaven" after all.

Jesus came to reveal the Father's love and make a way for us to understand: our Father's Heart, His desire to be in relationship with each of us, and His love and adoration for the nations. The only way we would be able to accept the truth of His Character was to see it demonstrated in person, and that person is Jesus Christ of Nazareth. We have stories of Jesus to read, the narrative of His demonstration of grace, His healing love. But we also have our own testimonies and stories of His demonstration and proof of the Father's love in our own lives. It simply takes a change of mind and letting Him change our hearts by breathing the Spirit of His Life into our weakened-by-sin spirits. We are given abundant (eternal) life if we ask for it.

But what about saying you're sorry for all your sins? What about confessing that you're a sinner, and displaying remorse over your wretchedness? What about praying the sinner's prayer? What about repentance? Repent for the Kingdom of God is here, right? Absolutely right!

As much as the word repentance has been used to describe feeling sorry or regretful for one's actions or sins, its original meaning is to change one's mind, or how you think about something. I read once that repentance actually can mean to follow a different king or ruler, to change your allegiance, to change your allegiance from one king to the new conquering king, to turn from one way of doing things toward doing something else, and to be baptized into a new way of living with a new government in charge. Baptism was a common ritual performed in all kinds of belief systems in New Testament times. It simply meant you were converting to a new system, a new way of believing, or committing your allegiance to a different leader. Repentance can also mean to stop being loyal to one ruler and transfer your loyalty to another. So who rules you?

Sometimes, our loyalty is strictly to ourselves. We are king of our own castles. Sometimes we look outside ourselves and follow other people we admire or idolize. But all too often we have been deceived by our culture or family traditions, and we become loyal to keeping superstitious rituals, and can even end up controlled by them, immersed in religious regulations, affected by mistaken ideas and misguided man-made rules. Our jaded view of Father God causes us to be loyal to legalism, thinking that somehow it will "appease His wrath."

CHAPTER 11: Is it Time to Stretch?

When it comes to repentance, if we look beyond the definition of remorse and regret and stretch our thinking to include a change of direction or allegiance, "Repent, for the Kingdom of God is at hand," would then be another way of saying "Get ready to change your allegiance from following impulses, old ways, listening to religious spirits, and open yourself up to being renewed and healed by Your Maker, the Lover of your soul. The Kingdom of God is here. Change your allegiance to Him."

I didn't want to pass on misinformation to you (if that definition of repentance was not accurate) so I researched and found that the Greek word translated as "repent" means "a change of mind." In the Old Testament, the Hebrew word translated as repent means "turn away from." But I really liked that "change of allegiance" idea, so next I looked up synonyms for that phrase and found some very interesting matches. Among them were: change of mind, rebirth, renewal, revival, and redemption. Would you agree that spiritual repentance causes renewal, rebirth, revival and redemption? Changing your thinking, stretching your mind, turning from mistaken ideas to something new, something significantly different, can bring all kinds of spiritual endorphins. I like that kind of stretching. I started writing this nine months ago. Do you think this pregnant pause that the whole world is in, could be God's way of stretching us?

I wonder if this is what a wineskin feels like when new wine is being poured into it.

CHAPTER 12: Wait, What Did That Say?

Asking for directions is hard enough; following them is a whole other story. My dad was a fourth-grade public school teacher for 38 years. One of the first assignments that he would give to his incoming students was a following-directions quiz. The first direction was always: "Be sure to read everything on this page before trying to complete these steps." Steps 1-4 were very complicated and hard to do. But the last step simply said: "Skip steps 1-4 and bring this paper, with your name on it, to the teacher." Skipping over one simple direction can cause us a lot more stress and work than necessary.

Following directions by a manufacturer can save you many hours of frustration. Are you a person who doesn't mind the words "some assembly required?" Are directions, recipes, and diagrams your friends? Or do reading manuals and instructions make you feel like you're somehow cheating? Do they take all the fun out of the challenge

CHAPTER 12: Wait, What Did That Say?

of piecing something together like a master puzzle-builder? Where is the creativity in following instructions, you ask?

I guess it really depends on the importance of whatever I'm assembling being well-constructed, as to whether or not I wing it. I may just look at the diagrams. But if it's important enough I'll read the words as well. For instance, if a child's safety is at risk (like if I was putting together a swing set), I'm going to probably pay close attention to both the illustrations and written directions. Plus, swing sets have, I think, at the minimum 50,000 pieces that you actually need, and then they throw in at least 10 that don't really go anywhere. They just sadistically throw them in to force the assembler to read the directions and look at the pictures that they spent the time and money to produce.

Following instructions, rules, or guidelines can be especially difficult if you feel they somehow stunt your freedom, make no sense, seem meaningless, or go against your vision. It can be hard to be cooperative, or even open to other ideas and opinions, and the way other people see things, when they are so different than yours. As a writer and director of stage productions, I was often on the giving end of directions. What I discovered, after a few frustrating years of things not turning out quite like I had hoped, was that envisioning and producing scripts and curriculum, unlike writing a book, takes a whole crew of people, all working together, acting it out and adding their own ideas to make something on paper into a reality. No matter what it is I envisioned, I could not make it happen on my own. I needed a team of people. I had to be able to paint the picture with words (and sometimes scribbled drawings) to help others see what I saw.

But we all see things from our own perspectives, don't we? We can even perceive shades of the same color a little differently. Is it a blueish green, or a greenish blue? Are you serious? No way! Purple? You're kidding, right? You really think it's purple?

Watching my vision performed differently than I had originally imagined it, because others added their own spin on it along with spontaneous adlibs, led me past frustration to the point of finally discovering that it actually made it more meaningful and richer. Validating and valuing each other's visions and ideas brought stage productions to a whole new level. I learned to love the team effort and whatever was produced more than what "could have been."

I think the vision God gave me was the target we needed to shoot for in order to produce what the team would actually make together. God knew what it would take. It was a beautiful thing. It was a training ground that helped me learn to aim for what I perceived as excellent, embrace the effort and any imperfections along the way, and to appreciate the process and the people more than the product. Truth is, I couldn't have done it without them. It's one of the ancient building blocks, a treasure of our past stored away in the old attic trunk — interdependence. We're like barn raisers, everybody doing their thing, working together to benefit the well-being of a community by creating something together.

CHAPTER 12: Wait, What Did That Say?

God gave me a helpful vision the other morning. I saw, from His eye-view, circles of people dancing, holding hands. Each circle was a different size and moving in opposite directions from the circle next to them, nearly touching and intertwining at certain spots, like the gears of a clock or a music box. Each person had to be there or the motion would come to a halt because each dancing gear intersected with another, and each person was needed in order to keep all the gears turning. It was as if God was showing me, it's time:

It's time for each circle of My people, large and small, all rejoicing, laughing, dancing, worshipping, some headed clockwise, others counter-clockwise; it's time for ALL my people to see how I see them: each gear an integral part, each tooth absolutely necessary to make My Church function. You may be headed in opposite directions from the community of believers next door, but you need each other to keep momentum and My purposes alive. Those gears have gotten rusty, and some loose screws have fallen into spots and worn down the mechanism. But I have removed debris and secured you now. I've sent the oil of my Holy Spirit to wash away the rustiness and cause the gears to turn again. But I need all of you. Not just "all of you" meaning "every person," but the all of every person, wholeheartedly surrendered to the direction I have for them to run; turning in synchrony, enjoying and laughing together, as they join hands and worshipfully dance, knowing they are each essential to My big picture and the purpose I created them for at this very moment in time.

I don't know if you have heard the phrase, "if you were the only person on the planet, Jesus still would have died for you." It's often spoken to someone who is feeling unimportant or unloved by God.

Be on Your Way

Somehow that phrase has never sat right with me. I know Scripture says Jesus endured the cross for the joy set before Him. I don't think saving just me would have provided Him enough incentive to endure the agony and shame He suffered. Here, see for yourself what Hebrews 12:1-3 is actually saying. It follows Chapter 11 which describes the incredible faith it took for so many of the Old Testament characters to accomplish their part of the story. They pressed through the drama and tragedies of life without actually experiencing the epic finale. They could only be sure of what they hoped for and certain of what they could not see. Their chapter ends with the words, "These were commended for their faith, yet none of them received what had been promised. God had planned something better for us so that only together with us would they be made perfect." Hebrews 12 continues:

> Therefore, since we are surrounded by such a great cloud of witnesses, let us throw off everything that hinders and the sin that so easily entangles, and let us run with perseverance the race marked out for us. Let us fix our eyes on Jesus, the author and perfecter of our faith, who for the joy set before him endured the cross, scorning its shame, and sat down at the right hand of the throne of God. Consider him who endured such opposition from sinful men, so that you will not grow weary and lose heart.

I'm here, and you're here, to make perfect (complete) the story that Abel, Enoch, Noah, Abraham, Sarah, Moses, Rahab, David, and so many others started. They all died looking forward to what God had

CHAPTER 12: Wait, What Did That Say?

promised them. Theirs was the prequel which set us up for these final chapters of the saga we're now living out: *Man Tries to Govern Himself*. And we're here to help write and set up the sequel epic adventure: *The Return of the King*. We're here to finish their story and perhaps witness with our own eyes the ultimate fulfillment of the joy set before each of them: the second return and long-awaited reign of Messiah King Jesus from Jerusalem!

But am I, alone, worthy to be considered the joy set before Jesus? Could I alone have compelled Him to endure the Cross? I don't think so. In fact, my real response (and probably yours) is "Of course not!" I've wondered about it for so long, that it found its way into this book. Wait, what did He just say? ... Oh, how I wish I could find the words to describe the sweetness of this moment. After years of asking, He just answered me. As I paused to hear what I should write next, I clearly heard Jesus' say:

I wouldn't have died with just you in mind.
But I wouldn't have died without you. You complete My joy.

That so resonates, doesn't it? I am a vital part, as are you, of Jesus' joyful reward — His Bride. Yet, we are also His brothers and sisters, adopted by our Father with His Blood. We have become His Blood relatives. Our spiritual DNA has been supernaturally rearranged to once again reflect our Heavenly Father's. Amazing! It's like God used everything we experience in human relationships of love to communicate and illustrate His indescribable, supernatural love for us. A book in the Old Testament entitled Song of Songs (or sometimes

Be on Your Way

Song of Solomon) describes this complex relationship we have with our God. We are described as a chosen people (Israel), a sister, as well as a lover and bride. This allegory is written with such uniquely descriptive ancient poetry and transparent layers that it helps us see the complicated but pure passion of our God for us individually and all together as a whole. If you're familiar with the book, you may recognize its influence in the poem God spoke to me a while back, as I wrestled with the question of God's individual love for just me. Why would He love *me?*

"You're Just Mine"

You have a special place in My heart. I constructed and formed you to be exactly who you are. I'm not going to love you anymore when I'm done with you than I do right now. I love you perfectly and completely.
This shape I see when I look at you, I've seen from the beginning of time.

I wanted you to be part of the process because by your making choices, My voice becomes clearer to you. I want you to not just know My voice, but to love My voice, to melt at My voice.

Can you hear Me knocking on your door, with My hand dripping in fragrant myrrh? No need to run to find your robe. Just come to the door as you are —
unashamed, excited to see Me, and eager to be embraced and loved,
just as you are.

I see only in you what I adore and cherish. Nothing more, nothing less. Sweet fragrances of prayers prayed — a culmination of divine and selfish, melding into transformed, pristine requests of desire and complete surrender.

CHAPTER 12: Wait, What Did That Say?

Let Me show you the way to wholeness and rest. Surrender to My true, tender strength, never to overpower you, but to lift you up to new heights and visions.

I am calling you. Will you, like the Shulamite bride, longingly look for Me, come after Me, and let Me carry you over the threshold into a brand-new place of intimacy with Me?

Don't be embarrassed by My love language. Don't be afraid of being rejected. Before you were born, I chose you. I shaped you to be the very person you are — My Beloved, forever accepted, admired, and loved.

You are My delight. All I want for you is for you to understand the relationship I intend to have with you, to reignite in you what was once shared in the Garden. Before the choice was made to live without My influence — without My wisdom and instruction — you knew Who you belonged to. You trusted Me because you could see Me as I really am.

Come My Dear One, let Me wipe the seeds of sleep from your eyes so you can see clearly the love I have for you in Mine. I long for you to look into My eyes and see them smiling, even dancing, with adoration for you. They are not angry, disappointed, or glaring. If you look closely enough, you will see your own reflection in My eyes, and you'll see what I see — a child who fills a Father's heart with joy, pride, and delight.

It's not that you're perfect; you're just Mine. I made you.
And as you know, everything I make is good. I never make a mistake.
I'll say it again ... I made you. I chose you. You did not choose Me.
No need to try to impress Me or hide things I already know about.
There is no fear in love.

Be on Your Way

My perfect love drives out all fear, because fear has to do with punishment. The one who fears has not been made perfect in love.[13] My love makes you perfect. Take My word for it. Believe it. I can't lie. I see you as perfect through My eyes of love.

Living in these complex family dynamics together is how we complete His vision — His epic stage production which is set, directed, lived and acted out under His divine direction. But God enjoys it when we adlib (He expects us to) as long as we don't get too far off track. He's the Director of this production. He picked this part just for you. In fact, He wrote the script with you in mind. So just be you and have fun with it.

I was given a little wooden, Swiss-chalet music box that, when opened, exposes the gears and workings inside, leaving me fascinated and wondering who thought to create such an ingenious thing. The tune it plucks out is sweet and makes me happy. You wind the key, open the rooftop lid, and everything inside starts moving and making the music it was designed to play. Shut the roof and it falls silent. The key has been wound, and God is wanting to lift the lid and unveil the beauty and ingenious works of His Creation, His Church.

---

[13] See 1 John 4:8

CHAPTER 12: Wait, What Did That Say?

Not only is He lifting off the roof, He's asking us to knock down the walls with Him. He did not intend those walls to be there. We're the ones who built the walls over time. We are not meant to worship only in a sanctuary. We're meant to make wherever we are, wherever we live, a sanctuary of worship. We are created to live, breathe, and worship every second of our lives, and gather with others who understand, who are willing to join hands, and walk (or dance) with us, celebrating together the awesomeness of our God. And we are asking those who don't know the Father's love yet to join the circle and dance like they belong — because they do (they just don't know it yet). No hoops to jump through, just hands to hold.

God needs us to say *yes*. He needs each circle of people, each tribe, to rise up; each person, each tooth of each gear, to be polished, oiled and ready to work together no matter what. Every circle, every gear, big or small, needs to be all-in, and loving God with all their hearts. That is only possible by individually experiencing God's love and realizing the delight He takes in living life within each of us. He delights in you. You did not choose Him. He chose you. Receiving His love is the only way we can truly love Him back, love ourselves, and faithfully love our neighbors.

But how? How does this all fit together? There are so many parts and pieces in the box. Sounds like this one might require reading and closely following both the Manufacturer's written directions *and* the illustrations. This one actually requires a whole Book of them. Just remember, life is like a swing set. There are too many pieces in the box, and life is too important to just wing it. The enemy throws in stuff you don't really need just to mess with you. So be sure to read everything in the Manual's pages before trying to pull it all together.

Step 1: Turn to Genesis – "In the beginning God created…"

Step 2: Keep reading.

Step 3: Don't stop till you reach Revelation 22:21…

"The grace of our Lord Jesus Christ be with you all. Amen."

CONCLUSION: Is This It?

When the ride becomes especially long, and as long as you're not the one driving, closing your eyes and letting sleep rescue you from the mundaneness of the journey can make arriving at your destination seem almost instantaneous. The car stops, we wake up blinking with blurry eyes, and through a groggy yawn ask, "Are we here?" Clearly, the answer is yes. We're not someplace else ... are we? Chances are you've probably asked that question at least once. Are we here? As philosophical as we can make them sound, there are times we ask seemingly very silly questions, even obvious ones. But in actuality, every question, if asked sincerely (even the "silly" ones), can serve a purpose. This is what I've discovered about asking lots of questions, especially when walking into unknown territory: The story told in the questions asked can open us up to all kinds of wonderment, and that in itself can change us for our good. Unanswered questions

CONCLUSION: Is This It?

actually hold more value by building our faith while teaching us to practice patience. They offer us opportunity to grow, more than getting a quick explanation or answer would. To live in the state of perpetual wonderment is a fascinating, awe-inspiring, and beneficial place to live. At least that's what I keep telling myself when I get frustrated and impatient because I'm not getting my questions answered fast enough, and this ride to who-knows-where is taking forever! Aren't we there *yet?*

God knows I do not care for unresolved mysteries or cliffhangers in the least. I despise those words at the end of a show, "To be continued…" To me it's like the tension caused by a suspended chord in a song that hangs you in midair and keeps you dangling there for what can feel like an eternity. The very word "suspense" causes knots to form in my shoulders. I can't let my shoulders down until it resolves into that beautiful, harmonious chord that follows and makes everything right and good again. So to ask questions and not get answers can definitely cause me stress. Hopefully, you're the kind of person who enjoys perpetual wonderment. If not, there's always the option to nap.

I feel like we have all been snoozing through the last part of this long, long journey, and the car just stopped and jarred us awake, "Is this it, God? Are we finally here?" For many, we've awakened before, but to disappointment because the answer has been, "No not yet. It's just a stop sign." To be honest, not having more answers by now to offer you has me wondering, "God, is this all You wanted me to write?

Be on Your Way

Is this really it?" God graciously led me to a verse in 1 Samuel to let me know His answer. The backdrop of the verse is the story of the prophet Samuel. We find Samuel very disappointed and grieving the prideful fall of Israel's very first king; a king whom the prophet had anointed and invested in both spiritually and emotionally. Tragically, King Saul grievously sinned and Samuel was bearing the bitter regret and disappointment of his failure. Then, 1 Samuel 16:1 continues:

> The Lord said to Samuel, "How long will you mourn for Saul, since I have rejected him as king over Israel? Fill your horn with oil and *be on your way*; I am sending you to Jesse of Bethlehem. I have chosen one of his sons to be king."

Obviously, the *emphasis* is mine. I was so excited to see *be on your way* in the Bible. God used those words to tell Samuel not to look back. Something new was coming. There was to be a new anointing of someone else — a boy after God's own heart — a boy who would one day become not just any king ... but King David! Fill your anointing "horn with oil and be on your way." I had no idea the title God gave me for this book was first spoken to the prophet Samuel about moving on, shaking off the past and anointing the future. And suddenly, it was reconfirmed: This *is* it!

God loves to speak to us in response to our curiosities. He dictates ideas and downloads answers into our lives all the time. Think of all those "Ah-ha!" moments. You didn't just come up with them. Neither did I. He uses His Word, and often times other people, to pour into us. But He also presents to us some incredible mysteries, puzzles, and

CONCLUSION: Is This It?

riddles along the way that at times will completely baffle us. Maybe we've grown just too tired to care, so we find ourselves shrugging, oh well, I guess we must be meant to live with unanswered questions. And, in some cases, that is true. But God really encourages us to keep seeking and knocking, and to stay curious. We ask, and then we listen — opening ourselves up to new ideas and possibilities that God wants to share with us. By persistently asking our questions, we can actually create a beautiful story (the story of a process) even though it may or may not come to a final conclusion within the time-frame of the telling, or in this case: the writing. Even though these chapters didn't reveal to me all the details of what God has for us to experience next, and I can almost hear a suspended chord playing in the background, the process of asking the questions and writing this all down not only gave me something to do while I was waiting, but has made me expectant, almost excited, and more ready. We need to be open to God's new strategies and revelations in order to get where He's taking us.

It heartens me to think that Jesus' disciples asked the same kinds of questions we tend to ask. Even though they were face to Face with the Son of God, it all still felt very unsure and mysterious to them. We see in John 14:1-9, as Jesus was comforting His friends, two sincerely asked inquiries were made of Him. It's interesting that He was the one about to head to the Cross, yet He's the one doing the comforting:

"Do not let your hearts be troubled. You believe in God; believe also in me. My Father's house has many rooms; if it were not so, I would have told you. I am going to prepare a place for you. And if I go and prepare a place for you, I will come back and take you to be with me that you also may be where I am. You know the way to the place where I am going."

Thomas said to him, "Lord, we don't know where you are going, so how can we know the way?"

Jesus answered, "I am the way and the truth and the life. No one comes to the Father except through me. If you really know me, you will know my Father as well. From now on, you do know him and have seen him."

Philip said, "Lord show us the Father and that will be enough for us."

Jesus answered: "Don't you know me, Philip, even after I have been among you such a long time? Anyone who has seen me has seen the Father …"

Of course, the disciples' future is our 20/20 hindsight. Yet even so, with their story in front of me, and God's Holy Spirit living within me, I still asked God similar questions back in the introduction of this book: "Be on my way to where? I have no idea where You're even taking us. How can I write about how to get there?" It's as if His response to me was the same He gave to Philip and Thomas: "Don't you know Me, Susan, even after I have been among you such a long time? I *am* the way."

CONCLUSION: Is This It?

And so began my writing trek of asking curious questions. As we come to the conclusion of what feels practically like a nine-month pregnancy — a time of waiting expectantly, feeling the aches and pains, the strain of carrying these weighty questions, but also the excitement and anticipation of what comes next — I feel as if this might be the transitional phase (the part where we bear down and push through). A woman in labor may have read all the books and may have an entire team of help beside her: a coach, a doctor or midwife, and the support of family and loved ones, but when it comes time to deliver, she is the only one pushing through the pain. We may all be in this together, supporting one another by encouraging, even coaching those around us, but when it comes to giving birth to this miracle God has planted in each of us, we must individually push through our personal pain. This book has been a record of the labor so far, and now it's time to bring that fragile little first-born home, and like any new parent the question we hear ourselves asking is, "Oh, God, now what?"

It was the same question I asked Him at the beginning of every chapter, looking to Him for directions, for clarity and wisdom as to what to write next. And before I knew it, here we are. This is as far as He's taken me. The time has come to release these suggestions and ideas into the world in hopes that you can combine them with what He's been showing you as well, connect all the pieces together, and build a beautiful mosaic on each other's foundational experiences, God-given gifts, and heaven-sent strategies.

Be on Your Way

All I can say is, "Thank you for coming along for the ride." We may be in different circles, traveling in different directions, maybe even on different sides of the world, but if you've confessed with your mouth that Jesus is your Lord, and you believe in your heart that God raised Him from the dead, then we are connected and synchronized by the Master Designer Himself. Our circles intersect at precise points, and we need each other to build momentum and get these wheels turning.

It brings me back to what started this whole book-writing endeavor: my vision of the Church on wagon wheels. I'm amused at the thought, because we're crossing into new territory, all moving together like pioneers and all I can think is: "Wagons Ho!" It just makes me smile. If you've heard the call (maybe not Wagons Ho, but to be on your way) and you're replying, "Where to, God? Just lead the way!" then this epic adventure together is just getting started. Be excited. This promises to be quite the trip!

Polished like an arrow in the shadow of My hand;
Made to claim my Kingdom back. It's time for you to stand —

And be on your way.

About the Author

For the past 30 years, Sue and her husband, Steve, have served in church leadership and ministry. She is a mother of two and a grandmother of five. She and Steve lived in central Massachusetts until 2014 when they moved to be near family in Connecticut. As lifelong New Englanders, their passion has always been to see God's Kingdom break ground in the very unique and often hardened soil of New England.

Sue has been creatively writing her whole life. Her ability was recognized early on by her teachers who unexpectedly presented her with a creative writing award at graduation. And though she did not pursue writing as a career, she did not let her gift go to waste. Over the years, she has been encouraged by many to publish her works of stage productions, children's church-curriculum, and live sermon illustrations (dramatic and comedic sketches), but the timing just didn't seem right to her — until recently.

God directed her to publish her first book (*Get Back on the Horse? GOD, You Can't Be Serious!*) in October 2019. After miraculously surviving childhood cancer, marrying her high school sweetheart, raising a daughter and son, ministering 25 years in different capacities at a local church, enduring seven years of care-giving for her parents (her mom having Alzheimer's); after being molded by some very

About the Author

traumatic life events, and then living through the pain of being pulled out of a very close-knit, conservative church family to pursue the supernatural gifts and calling of the Holy Spirit; after all of that, Sue was finally ready to publish her work. *Get Back on the Horse?* included many of her previous works, but turned out to be a culmination of the healing and recovery process God had laid out for her to walk through one page at a time.

Then just before publishing it, she woke up one morning to a dream-like vision of a church building rolling by on wagon wheels and hearing only the title, *Be on Your Way,* she knew she needed to begin writing her second book. With no idea where the book (or God) was taking her, she listened chapter by chapter for God's dictation, and wrote down what she thought she heard; nine months of writing later, it was complete (June 2020). Just days after publishing it, she heard the title of her next book: *What Now? From Dreading to Dreaming,* which then led to writing the sequel: *What Next? From Dreaming to Becoming.* Once more upon completion, another book title emerged: *Then What? Beyond the Dream,* and Sue knew it would complete the series…

at least for now.

Available at Amazon.com

Get Back on the Horse?

GOD, You Can't be Serious!

Life is hard. So is the ground. One minute you're whistling along and then, BAM! As if time skipped a beat without telling you, you're lying there in disbelief, praying if you don't try to get up maybe nothing will hurt. But the ground feels so much harder than it used to, and it looks like your boot straps are all but worn out. We all can use a hand up once in a while.

This collection of encouraging stories, scripts, poems, and prayers is meant to breathe life into weary travelers and give a leg up to those who know it's time to get back on the horse (even though the saddle seems too high off the ground).

If you think for now, you'd just rather walk, be assured you're not alone. And with each step taken and each page turned, you're that much closer to being ready to mount up again…

but this time with wings as eagles.

What Now?
From Dreading to Dreaming

Maybe it's the time of year, the time of life, or maybe it's just the weather, but somewhere along the way, the first few minutes of the day went from waking up from a dream to waking up into dread.

The battle is real for many of us. We wake up with an overwhelmingly heavy heart even though there really isn't anything worthy of dread on our daily agenda. What's that all about? When did our "what now?" turn into expecting the worst-case scenario instead of anticipating the sweet possibilities of what's next?

It only takes replacing one letter in "dreading" to turn it into "dreaming" again. Could it be that simple? It's time to get to the root of it all and find out. Are you with me?

Okay then ... What Now?

What Next?
From Dreaming to Becoming

You were actually designed and created to make *God's* dream come true. This sequel to *What Now? From Dreading to Dreaming,* was written to take us beyond dreaming by ourselves to a place of becoming what God is envisioning. He knows we can't do this alone. As long as there are negative voices and cynical dream crushers causing doubt, there will be the need for strategy, positive reinforcement, and the support of fellow dreamers.

God is about to resurrect the pieces of our individual forgotten dreams and somehow weave them all together, connecting all the dots in between dreamers to reveal His grander more glorious game plan. Believe it or not, we are all part of His "Dream Team," but He needs our cooperation. What do you say? Are you in?

Okay, then... What Next?

Then What?

Beyond the Dream

This book is written to all the followers of Jesus Christ who have dared enough to blaze a trail around old systems and climb their way over rocky paradigms because they know there is a higher calling and an elevation of God's Kingdom perspective that must be explored. He is calling those with ears to hear to arise from the ashes of a burned-out religious institution and to come discover their part in His strategic plan. We are about to step *beyond* the dream we have been carrying, because waiting for us at the top is something so amazing, it's beyond our imagination.

Are you at least a little curious to see what awesome views and miraculous experiences God has for us just ahead? The climb has made us stronger and ready. We are about to conquer the mountain. God's glorious destiny is just steps away.

Okay, but... Then What?

Made in the USA
Middletown, DE
25 October 2023